W9-CNA-127

Bull Terriers excel in agility competition.

This trio of Bull Terrier puppies pose for posterity.

HISTORY of the Bull Terrier

The purebred white Bull Terrier is descended from the cross between the Bulldog and the white English Terrier. Previously known as the Bull and Terrier, these dogs were not known for their beauty. They were famous for their gameness in the catting pits or in the sport of bull baiting and, sadly, also for their competition against each other in the fight ring. These first Bull and Terriers were often forced to fight until one or both died. These dogs had the stamina of the Bulldog and the intelligence of a terrier. They were quite leggy and quick, with agility for movement and turning. The first Bull Terrier was quite ugly, with a short thick head, blunt muzzle, and a thick heavy body. His strong jaw held an opponent as if in a vice.

In the early 1850s, Mr. James Hinks of Burmingham, England, startled the followers of the breed by crossing his dogs with the Dalmatian, Bulldog, and White Terrier. He introduced an entirely new breed. It was an immaculate, white-coated dog that was smaller, more elegant, and more pleasing to look at. He named it the Bull Terrier.

The baby pups in these litters were usually piebald or snowbald in color. The pups with the most white were kept for future breedings. In time these were mated to each other until, at last, Mr. Hinks was able to produce an all-white puppy that was able to produce pure-white puppies in succeeding generations. The Birmingham dogs showed a refinement and

It is believed that the Bull Terrier is the end result of crossing the original Bull and Terrier with the Dalmatian, Bulldog, and White Terrier.

grace that was absent from the mongrel Bull and Terrier. The bow legs, colored patches, coach backs, and undershot jaw were eliminated. This version of the Hinks' Bull Terrier was longer and cleaner in head, stronger in muzzle, and possessed more of a Roman finish at the end of the nose. This dog was also longer in neck, free from lippiness and thick throat, and more active.

This milk-white dog became the fashion of the

The pure milk-white Bull Terrier originated in the 1850s in Burmingham, England, showing a refinement and grace not seen before in the breed.

day, combining Bulldog tenacity with terrier grace. The extra length of muzzle proved to be an advantage in the fighting pit, giving the dog more strength of jaw and more holding power.

The claim was made that Hinks' dogs looked good but would not fight well in the pit. Hinks, however, had been very careful to keep breeding for gameness; he had no interest in breeding show dogs. He bred from only the gamest. He was always ready with 40-pound Puss, whom he matched against a 60-pound Bull and Terrier, owned by Mr. Tupper. Puss held the 60-pounder, winning the match. Puss then astonished the English show world by appearing the next day at the Holborn Dog Show and winning a red ribbon. There was not a mark on her glorious white coat.

One unusual aspect of the personality of the Bull Terrier is that the dog, supremely strong, fast, thoroughly game, and able to think, would not, even in pain, turn on his master. The standard states that the dog should have "character—full of fire, but amenable to discipline." This characteristic makes the breed unusually reliable with children, whose rough-housing could make a less friendly dog snap. When the Bull Terrier's patience is worn thin, he will just get up and move away.

The story is told that Ch. Rebel of Blighty, owned by Cabot Briggs, once lost his patience with a Pekinese that was insistent on fighting. He simply picked up the small dog and dropped it,

7

unharmed, into a wastebasket. The dog developed by Mr. Hinks is not quarrelsome as some overbred types may be. The Hinks' Bull Terrier was bred of sound mind and was slow to anger.

THE COLORED VARIETY

While Mr. Hinks was introducing his White Bull Terriers, the colored dog Jacko was doing his rat killing in the pits. In the 1840s, ratting was a gory game played by the "gentlemen of the sport." They pitted their Bull Terriers against the rats. One little black-and-tan-colored terrier called Jacko weighed only 13 pounds. He killed 60 rats in 2 minutes, 40 seconds; 100 in 5 minutes, 28 seconds; and 1000 in 100 minutes.

However, the bloody sport was beginning to be looked down upon by the breeders. It soon started to disappear to the darkest corners, into out-of-the-way barns and hidden alleys. The Colored Bull Terriers were not recognized by the Kennel Club until 1935. Then they were called Staffordshire Bull Terriers. The White Bull Terrier of Mr. Hinks' creativity and these square-jawed dogs (today's Staffordshire Bull Terrier) existed alongside each other. Both were called the Bull Terrier. At the time the breed was created, interbreeding these two species was not uncommon, being only a few generations apart. But in the years to follow, they would become two distinct breeds.

In the early 1900s, a band of dedicated breeders began breeding Coloreds along the lines of the White Bull Terrier. This was to be a long hard effort. Faced with the opinion of some of the breeders of the time that the Colored variety was despised by the fancy, the fanciers of the Colored had their work cut out for them.

The Bull Terrier made his first appearance in the United States in the early 1900s. Ch. Ann Dee's Blackstone Benny.

Today's Bull Terriers come in a vast array of colors, including brindle, black and white, and tri-color. Litter owned by Mitch Woodlief.

The Colored variety owed their heritage to two breeders, E. A. Lyon of London and H. J. L. Tummer of Doneaster. They began their task in 1907. Mr. Lyon had used colored dogs of the old black-and-tan kind in India to hunt jackals. Using the prefix of Sher, his dedication to the betterment of the Colored progressed. However, Mr. Lyon's Bull Terrier strain was small in stature, with color, temperament, and gameness being of the most importance. He made little progress in head type or substance. Later on, Mr. Lyon would be of importance in the breeding of the Miniature Bull Terrier. He continued to breed Coloreds until the beginning of World War II. He became an enthusiast of the Romany Kennels after the war. It was his persistence during the early days in establishing the brindle coat that gave Mr. Lyon a place in the history of the Colored Bull Terrier.

Bing Boy was the first Colored to win a Challenge Certificate at the Great Joint. Outraged that the judge would put a Colored over the top White dog of the day, the Bull Terrier Club filed a protest against awarding Bing Boy his special prizes. A letter, dated February 12, 1920, was sent to the Kennel Club. It asked that the Coloreds and the Whites be formed into two separate varieties, with the awarding of two separate Challenge Certificates. This was denied by the Kennel Club. To this day, Bull Terriers are still judged as one breed. Ironically, the United

States is the only country in the world where Bull Terriers are registered and shown as two separate varieties. All other countries register and exhibit them as one breed.

Bing Boy went on to gain another Certificate in the ring. He was to be used at stud widely. However, he had small impact on the progress of the breed. He did gain fame as the Colored who broke the White monopoly of the fanciers.

Today's Colored Bull Terriers owe much to the dedicated breeding program of the Romany Kennels, composed of Ms. D. Montague Johnstone and Mrs. Meg Williams. They were producing heads on their dogs in the 1950s and 60s. Most important, they produced Colored Bull Terriers that were being shown and winning. The impact of the Romany Kennels is still felt over 50 years later in the breed. A record stands today unbroken in the show ring with the Silverwood being won by one of their descendants, a Colored dog.

Some of the famous early Colored Bull Terriers that had impact on the breed are as follows: Jock of the Bushveldt, born in 1910, was a product of a Bulldog bred to a Manchester Terrier bitch. This dog is behind the early Colored Bull Terriers. Blue Cross Boy was the uncrowned champion of the war years. He took Best of Breed at the largest show during the war, "The Big Top" in July, 1944. It was very hard to continue breeding in England during the war, as petrol was rationed, along with tires. It was almost impossible to travel any length of distance to breed the dogs. It is fortunate that there were a few very good stud dogs available. Some very dedicated breeders were able to carry on their programs. One of the important war time stud dogs was Contango Consul, sire of Contango Cobblestone, who in turn sired Romany Rivet.

As the breed progressed in England, a lot of attention was beginning to focus on importing top dogs to America. Many of these imported dogs were White, with a few good Colored among them. The Colored added a lot of substance and redefined the heads. But it still was not acceptable to breed and show the Coloreds. In the late 1940s, the disdain of the Coloreds started to fade. More and more breeders looked to the Colored for quality. At that time, they were more of the terrier type and lent some style and flair to the cobbier Whites. Also, breeders were finding that interbreeding the Whites to the Coloreds was reducing the incident of deafness, which has plagued this breed from its conception.

At the Bull Terrier Club of America's (BTCA) annual general meeting in 1949, Herbert Stewart successfully moved and carried the motion:

"That the Club's Standard for the Bull Terrier shall henceforth be known and titled Standard of Perfection for the White Bull Terrier and the Standard of Perfection for the Colored Bull Terrier, as accepted and approved by the American Kennel Club, May 12, 1936, be accepted as the Standard of Perfection for the Colored Bull Terrier and that both standards be published by the Bull Terrier Club of America as the Standards of the Breed and that the American Kennel Club be notified of this action."

And so it began officially that the Colored could show. They first competed in the Colored classes at the 1949 Specialty in New York, where Brandywine Spitfire took Best of Variety.

Two of the most influential breeders in the late 1940s and early 50s were Mrs. Florence

The courageous Bull Terrier is well known for her steady temperament and loyalty to her master.

Gogarty and Dr. Edward S. Montgomery. Mrs. Gogarty had been a resister of the Colored. After going to England in 1948, and upon seeing how well the Colored had advanced in the breed, she returned to America with six Colored. One finished his championship in five shows. Dr. Montgomery at one point had the largest Bull Terrier kennels in the country at his Cabot, Pennsylvania, home. With his superb knowledge of breeding, he soon had many champions. One of his imports, the lovely brindle Romany Ritual, became the first Colored to win Best in Show at an all-breed show.

Once a fighting dog, the Colored Bull Terrier has eventually gained the same high qualities and virtues of his white-colored cousins.

The account of people who influenced the Colored progress would be remiss if the name of Mr. James Boland was not mentioned. He was a noted historian and advocator of the BTCA Specialty winner. His dog won Best of Variety at two back-to-back Specialties of the BTCA. This win is also noteworthy in that it is the first show where the varieties competed against each other for Best of Breed. This time it was won by a White. In 1954, the American Kennel Club decided that the varieties must meet for Best of Variety at any specialty show not held in conjunction with an all-breed show. This ruling still applies today. It should be noted that the first Colored champion to be recorded was Ch. Beltona Bringigal, a solid brindle owned by Willet McCortney.

The Colored Bull Terrier is available in quite a few colors: brindle white, solid brindle, black brindle, red smut, solid red, fawn, tricolor (black, white, and tan), black, and black and white. The standard states, however, that "when all things are

Throughout the years dedicated breeders have devoted themselves to the welfare and development of the Bull Terrier.

equal, brindle is the preferred color." Today's Colored Bull Terrier can compete with any Bull Terrier at any given show. The modern day breeders have bred for heads, bone, and substance. Temperaments are greatly improved from the "fighting" dog of yesteryear. The White and Colored Bull Terriers are on an even parallel. If one visits the next specialty show you will see the excellent quality that the dedicated breeder has produced.

THE MODERN BULL TERRIER

Today's Bull Terrier differs strongly from the early 1900 Bull Terriers. Bodies have gotten better and the dog now possesses a shorter back, straighter front, and better layback of shoulder. This gives the modern Bull Terrier a more balanced look.

There are three types of Bull Terriers today: the Terrier type, the Bully type, and the Dalmatian type, also known as the Middle of the Road type.

The Terrier type has quality, agility, and soundness. These are the primary virtues in the smaller compact dog. The Bully type must have substance, density, and heavy bone, which is exaggerated in this dog. The Dalmatian type has more leg, sweeping body lines, and a free long stride. The combination of these subtypes is essential for providing the genetic ingredients that produce the ideal combination of substance, soundness, and shapeliness called for in the Bull Terrier standard.

The spirited Bull Terrier's good temperament should be evident in his lively expression.

The modern Bull Terrier, while keeping the old fighting Bull and Terrier spirit, is no longer the ugly, ferocious, "Bill Sykes" dog that was bred for the pits. Today's dogs weigh between 45 and 70 pounds, some a few pounds more. The bitches weigh anywhere from 40 pounds to 60 pounds. Again, a few may weigh a bit less or a bit more. The ideal weight for a male is around 60 pounds. The ideal weight for bitches is around 52 pounds. There is no weight classification listed in the standard.

The smaller-bred animals are classified as Miniature Bull Terriers. They look like their bigger cousins, but the two are not to be interbred.

The current day Bull Terrier owes his pedigree to three or four great English champions: Brigadier, Vindicator, McGuffin, and Bar Sinister. Brigadier, Vindicator, and McGuffin were kings of their years, winning the Regent Trophy for 1937, 1938, and 1939, respectively.

Since World War II, body type has generally improved more than head type. In the last ten years though, heads have improved dramatically. Today's Bull Terriers in the United States can compete with any in the world.

The McGuffin-Vindicator combination produced many champions by breeding a McGuffin bitch to Vindicator, or to his son, the Knave of Romandy. Males of the McGuffin line bred to females of the Vindicator line also bred champions and

winners in rapid succession. The Bull Terrier is very spirited, but thanks to Mr. Hinks, he is well under control.

Considered a separate breed the Miniature Bull Terrier, shown here, is a smaller version of the Bull Terrier.

With powerfully built jaws of steel, the Bull Terrier is made much like a prizefighter ready for combat. He is conscious of his awesome power. He knows he cannot be downed physically. Such a dog has no need to indulge in false bragging or to demonstrate his toughness. He knows it is there, and it is there when he needs it. Only the bully or temperamentally unbalanced dog constantly needs to demonstrate his ferocity.

Stories of affection for children abound throughout Bull Terrier history. One of the stories in the late 1970s is about a white male champion named Lord Ashley. He saved his family from fire and possible death. In the wee hours of the night, he became aware of a hissing noise and smoke coming from his young mistress's bedroom door. He alerted the family by barking and scratching at her door until the father awakened and found that the electrical cord leading to a lamp was sparking and smoldering, ready to ignite into a fire.

Another story tells about a small 40-pound bitch named Lucy. She attacked and killed a huge Oklahoma rattlesnake that had crawled into the playpen of a two year old. Seizing the rattler, Lucy crushed it, but not before it had bitten her several times. This led to Lucy's death, but she saved the baby.

The Bull Terrier's strength and powerfully built features are all that remain from his days as a ferocious varmint killer.

The Bull Terrier makes a wonderful family companion and loyal guardian that relates well to children.

In Hawaii, we heard of the Bull Terrier male that caught the mugger who had stolen his mistress's purse. Also, there was the small white bitch named Stitches in West Virginia who sensed there was an intruder outside the window. She was let out the door. She grabbed the peeping tom, held him until the police arrived, and saved her mistress from possible harm. What a sight it must have been to see this 40-pound white fury hanging onto the leg of the cursing kicking intruder.

The stories are innumerable and they are important in the folklore of the Bull Terrier. They show that these dogs, pound for pound, can be as compelling and courageous as a bodyguard and still be an affectionate best friend. This is called "loyalty."

THE SILVERWOOD COMPETITION

In the late 1960s, a young couple by the name of Hope and Bill Colket had a dream of a great yearly competition for the best bred Bull Terrier in North America. Encouraged by Raymond Oppenheimber of the Ormondy Kennel in England, they began to lay the groundwork for such an event. Tragically, the Colkets were killed in two fatal car accidents within months of each other. The Bull Terrier Club of America decided to go ahead with the idea. The BTCA called it the Silverwood Competition, in honor of the Colkets, whose prefix was Silverwood.

The purpose of the Silverwood Trophy Competition is to provide a place to bring together the best specimens of the Bull Terrier breed in order to evaluate the animals for individual breeding programs. This purpose would only benefit those who participated in the showing and breeding. As the shows gained public attention, more and more exhibitors began breeding the best to the best. Some breeders have made the mistakes of breeding their bitches to the top-winning dog. This has not improved their show stock. The big winner is not for every bitch!

Fortunately, many people in the United States and Canada have taken advantage of this fantastic opportunity. As a result, they have greatly elevated the quality of the breed. The Silverwood has served as a place to see the best stock available and to share breeders' ideas and experiences.

The Silverwood Competition is for American-bred Bull Terriers. American-bred is defined as animals bred and whelped on the North American continent, Hawaii, or offshore

Ch. Ann Dee's Fire Chief Zodiac, ROM, was a finalist in the prestigious Silverwood Trophy Competition.

islands. The dog or bitch to be exhibited must belong to a member of the Bull Terrier Club of America. The trophy awarded is the top award, the Silverwood Trophy. It is a carved wood White Bull Terrier, crafted by Mr. Harris, a fine English carver. It was presented to the Bull Terrier Club of America by the Bull Terrier Club (England) in memory of Hope and Bill Colket. The award for Best of Opposite Sex was also

Only the best Bull Terriers are used for breeding in order to pass on good quality and temperament.

The overall appearance of the Bull Terrier should reflect power, endurance, agility, and animation.

presented to the BTCA by the Bull Terrier Club of England. It is a Nymphenberg porcelain figure of a White Bull Terrier. It is the Regent Trophy replica won by Eng. Ch. Raydium Brigadier in 1937. It was

willed to the Bull Terrier Club by his owner, Gladys Adlam. At the beginning of World War II, Mrs. Adlam exported Brigadier to the United States to Jessie Bennett's Coolyn Hill Kennels. Therefore, the Raydium Brigadier Trophy is awarded in memory of both Gladys Adlam and Jessie Bennett.

Beginning in 1972, the BTCA awarded a trophy to the runner-up of the Silverwood Trophy Winner. This award was dedicated in 1973 to the memory of Lavender Lovell and it has since been known as the Lovell Trophy. It is a Royal Doulton porcelain figure of a Colored Bull Terrier and a Royal Copenhagen porcelain figure of a White Bull Terrier bitch.

In 1977, the BTCA awarded a trophy to the breeder of the Silverwood Winner. It is the Ch. Bramblemer Gay Carolynda Trophy, in memory of George Pinque. It is awarded to any Bull Terrier Champion or one that wins Best of Variety (BOV), Best of Opposite Sex (BOS), Winners Dog (WD), Winners Bitch (WB) or reserve at a three-point Recognition of Merit (ROM) show or WD, WB, BOV, or BOS at a two-point ROM show. Any Bull Terrier may receive a special invitation from the BTCA Board of Directors. Requests must be made in writing and in video and are reviewed by the Board.

This competition is judged by three judges. They are selected by a judging committee that is appointed by the Board. Procedures are designed so that two judges must agree on any top placements or trophies awarded in the competition. If the two judges disagree, the referee judge will make the final decision.

The Silverwood has been held each year since 1970. In the 25 competitions held to date, only three have been won by the Colored variety. To date, the only Colored dog to win the Silverwood Trophy was Ch. Ann Dees Red Adair, ROM in 1979. This red-white dog's lineage goes back to the Romany Kennels, by way of the Hollyfir Kennels of Jack Mildenhall.

There have been two Colored bitches to win the Silverwood. The first was in 1983. It was a brindle-white, Ch. Westbrook Windborne. The second was in 1994, the brindle-white, Ch. Action Ragin Cagun, ROM.

The Silverwood Competition has caused breeders to make great strides in their breeding programs. But it also has caused some problems in the breeding of the dogs. Because everyone wants to breed the dog that will win the Silverwood, many breeders will take some very risky chances when selecting a mate for their bitch. Some have used dogs with exceptional heads, while ignoring structure, bad bites, and even poor temperaments. Thankfully, this is starting to wane. Breeders are becoming more aware of genetic problems. They realize that in every litter, there are more pet quality dogs than show quality.

There are some breeders that are still overbreeding. There was a time that Bull Terrier breeders would cull the litter. This seems to not be the case anymore. Breeders spend vast amounts of money at the vet's office to save all the puppies in the litter. No one can say whether this is a good practice or not. It seems there are homes for every pup, even the runt of the litter. As long as these puppies are placed into pet homes, with no breeding terms, this is satisfactory with no ill results to the breed.

Responsible breeders will provide homes for all the dogs produced in any litter.

CHARACTERISTICS of the Bull Terrier

The character of a Bull Terrier is so unique that there is no other breed of dog like him. Small or large, Bull Terriers are alike in their character. They are fun-loving dogs. They will meet every demand that an owner will put on them, from showing in the ring to simply being a couch buddy. They have been known to sniff for bombs in World War II in England and to herd sheep and goats in India. They have sailed on the oceans with sailors and walked the trenches with soldiers. They are known for their loyalty and undying love. They are tough little dogs and their appearance does not let the public forget what the original Bull Terrier was created for—to fight in the pits.

The Bull Terrier's love for children and seniors is uncanny. Stories abound about how the Bull Terrier has saved children from fires, found lost children, and saved older folks from drowning—done by a breed that most people think cannot swim! Bull Terriers are by nature busy dogs, especially as pups. As puppies, they do not like to sit still for anything. As they get older, they become more trainable. By the time they are four or five years old, the living room couch looks pretty inviting to them.

The Bull Terrier's attachment to children is legendary, and they enjoy participating in fun and games with gentle companions.

The standard states that "A Bull Terrier must be strongly built, muscular, symmetrical and active, with a keen, determined and intelligent expression, full of fire but of sweet disposition and amenable to discipline." This is asking a lot of a dog, and yet, this is what you will get in a Bull Terrier!

A lot of people think that a Bull Terrier is aloof and hard to train. He is not really aloof. He has a tendency to have a "wait and see" attitude. He can be very inquisitive, giving strangers a "checking you out" greeting. He will approach, do a sniff test, circle you with a few dancing steps, subject himself to your petting and back rubbing, then sit back and take a good look at the person who is being overly friendly. If he accepts you, be prepared for a few high jumps, and sometimes a few body

slams. Then he will sit as close to you as possible, usually ending up sitting on your feet, which they love to do!

As for training, they are ultra-smart; they just don't let you always see it. Do something one time with a Bull Terrier and it will be a lifetime thing. When they go to obedience school, most trainers immediately think they are pit bulls and want to muzzle them. Of course, the Bull Terrier does not want to be treated this way. He will misbehave, get excused, and be sent home. On the way home, his owner is crestfallen, but these dogs can learn obedience. You just have to have more patience with them.

When his fighting spirit is disciplined by his family loyalty, the Bull Terrier approaches the ideal pet. The danger is that he can become extremely jealous of a rival for his family's affection. Care

Although it may take time and patience, your Bull Terrier is very intelligent and can be trained to do anything. "Tessi," owned by Dorinda Desmet, excels in agility competition.

If you introduce your Bull Terrier to other pets in your household while he is still young, he will make friends that last a lifetime.

must be taken when there are other animals around. Bull Terriers can live with many animals, including members of their own breed. There are known breeders of the Bull Terrier who have multiple "Bullies" living in the house together. Bull Terriers have been known to live with cats, Rottweilers, rabbits, and even ferrets.

There are no perfect Bull Terriers. Today's Bull Terrier, though, is coming very close to the ideal. Temperament and soundness combined with beauty is available today, thanks to the superb breeding knowledge displayed by the modern breeder.

The Bull Terrier is not a breed meant for everyone. Many problems can arise after a pup goes into his new home. The pup may then be sent back to the breeder and branded as incorrigible. Sometimes, changing ownership will straighten out the pup's naughty behavior and he will adapt to his new family. Bull Terriers are a special breed for special people. With some beforehand knowledge and by working closely with your breeder, you can be one of those special people for these special dogs.

STANDARD for the Bull Terrier

The standard for the Bull Terrier appears below, followed by an explanation and dicussion of each section in italics. This standard was taken from the Bull Terrier Illustrated Standard published by the Bull Terrier Club of America in 1991. To obtain a copy of the full context of this standard, contact the American Kennel Club and ask for the name and telephone number of the Corresponding Secretary of the Bull Terrier Club. This copy of the standard holds numerous photos of the correct and incorrect points of the Bull Terrier and is an extraordinary copy for novices and judges of the breed.

The overall appearance of the Bull Terrier should be one of strength, balance, and intelligence.

WHITE

The Bull Terrier must be strongly built, muscular, symmetrical and active, with a keen, determined and intelligent expression, full of fire but of sweet disposition and amenable to discipline.

*The standard opens with a general description of a positive and charismatic dog. The Bull Terrier should be the maximum dog in the available space; a dense substantial animal, but with balance and agility. He should give the impression of strength, energy, and quickness. The expression should reflect these body projections: A positive, glinting, intelligent eye set in a triangular opening that produces a "varminty" look. Temperament is of the utmost importance in a Bull Terrier. He must be outgoing, friendly, interested in his surroundings, and on his toes, but **never** bad-tempered or shy.*

The head of the Bull Terrier should be clean cut, long, and deep, with a vivacious and animated expression.

Head–The head should be long, strong and deep right to the end of the muzzle, but not coarse. Full face it should be oval in outline and be filled completely up, giving the impression of fullness with a surface devoid of hollows or indentations, i.e., egg shaped. In profile it should curve gently downwards from the top of the skull to the tip of the nose. The forehead should be flat across from ear to ear. The distance from the tip of the nose to the eyes should be perceptibly greater than that from the eyes to the tip of the skull. The underjaw should be deep and well defined.

Lips–should be clean and tight.

Teeth–should meet in either a level or in a scissors bite. In the scissors bite the upper teeth should fit in front of and closely against the lower teeth and they should be sound, strong and perfectly regular.

Ears–should be small, thin and placed close together. They should be capable of being held stiffly erect when they point upwards.

Eyes–should be well sunken and as dark as possible, with a piercing glint and they should be small, triangular and obliquely placed; set near together and high up on the dog's head. Blue eyes are a disqualification.

Nose–should be black, with well-developed nostrils bent downward at the tip.

The overall shape and proportions of the Bull Terrier head are very important. It must have strength, be egg-shaped, and have piercing expressions for the animal to approach the ideal. From the side view, the head should demonstrate the clean, sweeping, unbroken profile called for in the standard and should also have depth and strength of muzzle and underjaw. From the front, the head should be egg-shaped, with no indentations from the base of the ear to the end of the muzzle. The end of the muzzle should be strong and broad. More strength of muzzle with less curve of profile is preferable to a pronounced profile with a narrow muzzle that tapers to a point.

The expression is a key feature of the Bull Terrier. Together with the dense, muscular, shapely body and correctly-shaped head, the "varminty" look is responsible for making the dog a Bull Terrier and not just a strong chunky dog.

The eye openings should be slanted and triangular, set relatively high in the head, with a dark keen eye. The ears add to the alert expression and should be close together and pointing upwards. A Bull Terrier with donkey ears and a round kind eye or a pale eye loses the intense, alert, "varminty" look so valued in the breed.

The teeth have become more of a problem as the profile has become more exaggerated. In order to accommodate a very curved (and somewhat shortened) nose profile, the underjaw has either remained deep, long, and broad, producing undershot dentition, or it has become narrow and shortened (pig-jawed). This allows the front incisors to meet in the preferred scissors, but crowds the lower canines inward where they can prevent the mouth from completely closing. The canines can damage or puncture the hard palate above. Premolars are often missing in Bull Terriers as well.

This is possibly a result of this progressive genetic shortening of the lower jaw to achieve a more exaggerated profile and retain a scissors bite. A deep strong underjaw can be appropriately balanced by a long wide muzzle with the correct profile to accommodate proper dentition.

Any mouth fault should be penalized only and precisely according to its degree. A proper assessment should include the strength and width of the underjaw, the size and regularity of the teeth, the severity of malocclusion, and the placement of the lower canines. The lower canines should be fully visible with the tops in front of the upper canines and outside of the upper gum. Inward displacement of the lower canines can be damaging to the dog as well as prevent correct closure of the upper and lower jaws.

The Bull Terrier's body should possess a short back, and well-knit strength with graceful lines.

Neck—should be very muscular, long, arched and clean, tapering from the shoulders to the head and it should be free from loose skin.

Chest—should be broad when viewed from in front, and there should be great depth from withers to brisket, so that the latter is nearer the ground than the belly.

Body—should be well rounded with marked spring of rib, the back should be short and strong. The back ribs deep. Slightly arched over the loin. The shoulders should be strong and muscular but without heaviness. The shoulder blades should be wide and flat and there should be a very pronounced backward slope from the bottom edge of the blade to the top edge. Behind the shoulders there should be no slackness or dip at the withers. The underline from the brisket to the belly should form a graceful upward curve.

The overall impression of the Bull Terrier's body should be one of short-backed, well-knit strength with graceful lines.

The topline should flow continuously from the base of the ears over a graceful neck, tying smoothly into the level withers and then back to a slight rise over a muscular loin, finishing in a gentle curve over the croup to a low-set tailhead.

A long, arched, tapering neck rising from a well-angulated shoulder is a valued component of the overall balance. The rib cage can be assessed easily from a top view, the sides of the dog curving outwards to accommodate the well-sprung ribs, and curving in behind the rib cage to make a discernable waist. The Bull Terrier should be a combination of dense but smooth parts connected by graceful curves.

Legs—should be big boned but not to the point of coarseness; the forelegs should be of moderate length, perfectly straight, and the dog must stand firmly upon them. The elbows must turn neither in nor out, and the pasterns should be strong and upright. The hind legs should be parallel viewed from

The Bull Terrier's tail should be short, low, and carried horizontally.

The hindquarters of a Bull Terrier must be well balanced and proportionate.

behind. The thighs very muscular with hocks well let down. Hind pasterns short and upright. The stifle joint should be well bent with a well-developed second thigh.

Feet–round and compact with well-arched toes like a cat.

The standard calls for straight front legs with elbows pointing straight back and the middle toes straight forward.

Tail–should be short, set on low, fine, and ideally should be carried horizontally. It should be thick where it joins the body and should taper to a fine point.

A properly set-on tapered tail, carried horizontally, gives a finish to the topline that is essential to our visualization of the ideal Bull Terrier.

Coat–should be short, flat, harsh to the touch and with a fine gloss. The dog's skin should fit tightly.

Color–is white, although markings on the dog's head are permissible. Any markings elsewhere on the coat are to be severely faulted. Skin pigmentation is not to be penalized.

While hair texture is not generally regarded as important in the overall picture of the ideal Bull Terrier, a thin, patchy, or dull coat detracts from the impression of a vibrant healthy animal. Coats marred by bouts of allergies are also a sign of less than ideal health, as well as unsightly. Ticking, which occurs in the undercoat, is more prevalent in the winter coats. This is a fault as described in the standard. The severity of the fault can be minimal, with a low add tick in the undercoat, or more penalized if the coat is heavily ticked. Mismarks, that are actual patches of color on the neck, body, or tail involving both the undercoat and the longer guard hairs, are also a fault that carries a penalty under the rules of the standard. Skin pigmentation, the dark spots on the skin that show through the white hair in a thin coat, is not to be penalized. It has been the practice when judging Bull Terriers to view light ticking and small mismarks as relatively minor faults in an otherwise worthy animal.

Ch. Skyhills Mad Mariah, ROM, owned by Betty Desmond, is a shining example of the breed.

Movement–The dog shall move smoothly, covering the ground with free, easy strides, fore and hind legs should move parallel each to each when viewed from in front or behind. The forelegs reaching out well and the hind legs moving smoothly at the hip and flexing well at the stifle and hock. The dog should move compactly and in one piece but with a typical jaunty air that suggests agility and power.

A Bull Terrier that is made well is likely to move well. It is in motion that the animal passes the true test of construction. From the front, the forelegs should be perfectly straight, with the feet the same distance

The Bull Terrier's coat should be short, flat, and harsh to the touch. Ch. Sinbar Black Onyx of Ann Dee, owned by Sandra Frascone and Betty Desmond.

32

apart as the elbows. If the shoulders and elbows are not properly constructed, the elbows will visibly turn outward, and the feet will be closer together than the elbows. Any deviations in the straightness of the forelegs will be noticeable. These are often accompanied by a "crossing" or "weaving" gait.

From the rear, the hind legs should also be parallel. Bowed-out stifles and hocks will cause the hind feet to turn in. They sometimes actually cross as the dog puts one foot in front of the other. Cowhocks, or hocks that turn in toward the center line, will cause the stifles and hind feet to turn out with a resulting loss of impulsion or drive.

From the side, animals with straight shoulders will usually show some slackness or a dip behind the withers. A straight hind leg and a badly made croup will cause the hind end to be higher than the front. This gives the impression that the animal is "running downhill."

Because the standing Bull Terrier can be cleverly "stacked" to minimize these basic construction problems, it is essential for breeders and judges alike to familiarize themselves with the ideal Bull Terrier in motion.

Faults—Any departure from the foregoing points shall be considered a fault and the seriousness of the fault shall be in exact proportion to its degree, i.e. a very crooked front is a very bad fault; a rather crooked front is a rather bad fault; and a slightly crooked front is a slight fault.

DISQUALIFICATION—*Blue eyes.*

It must be remembered that the Bull Terrier is first and foremost an active and energetic dog, and this should always be reflected in his conformation and temperament.

COLORED

The Standard for the Colored Variety is the same as for the White except for the subhead "Color" which reads: *Color*: Any color other than white, or any color with white markings. Other things being equal, the preferred color is brindle. A dog which is predominantly white shall be disqualified.

DISQUALIFICATIONS—*Blue eyes. Any dog which is predominately white.*

Your Bull Terrier's coat should always appear healthy and shiny. Ch. Ann Dee's Crimson Tide, owned by Jim Arrington, is an example of one of the acceptable coat colors.

Mc. Williams Never Offside, owned by Wil de Veer is only eight weeks old but already demonstrates the deliberate stance and powerful build of the Bull Terrier.

Bull Terriers *usually exhibit a degree of animation and individuality in the ring. They should not be penalized for their exuberant approach to life if they are not overly disruptive or aggressive, they should be under control at all times and be amenable to handling by the judge.*

SELECTING the Right Bull Terrier for You

Volumes could be written on this subject by different breeders and none of them would be the same. Most breeders have their own ideas as to what makes a perfect Bull Terrier. There is no "perfect" Bull Terrier, although each breeder or owner wants to think that his dog qualifies.

The first question you must ask yourself is: "Do I really want one of these dogs?" If the answer is "yes," the second question is: "Do I want to show my dog or do I only want a pet and companion?"

Be sure to do your homework and learn all you can about the breed before making the decision to bring a Bull Terrier into your home.

Your Bull Terrier will have a good start in life if his parents are happy and well adjusted. Make sure to see the dam and sire of the puppy you are considering.

While you are pondering these questions, it is best to go to the local library and read everything it has on the breed. Once you know what a Bull Terrier looks like, read about his characteristics, his needs, his care, and his health problems. Now you are ready to look for a breeder.

The best place to find a reputable breeder is through the corresponding secretary of the Bull Terrier Club of America. This person can put you in touch with breeders close to your area. You can find the name of the secretary by contacting the American Kennel Club. If you find your breeder by way of newspaper ads, it would be wise to check on the breeder first. Breeders also advertise in national dog magazines. These are usually a safe way of finding a puppy. Again, a word to the wise: Call several breeders and ask for references of the breeder with whom you are thinking of dealing.

Upon selection of your Bull Terrier puppy, the breeder should offer a guarantee against inherited disorders.

Since the "Spuds McKenzie" episode of several years ago, many backyard breeders appeared wishing to cash in on the popular dog. Owning a Bull Terrier will be a major purchase on your part. Go about it like a detective; make lots of contacts and inquiries.

Now you have found a breeder you wish to buy from. When going to look at the litter, ask to see the dam and the sire. If the sire is not on the premises, ask for photos of him, a health certificate, and a pedigree. Ask for the name of the sire's owner and a phone number where he can be located. This is important. If some illness or trait comes up later on, it would help to know if the sire had the same thing. The breeder also can help you select a puppy for either show or as a pet.

You may be buying your puppy from a breeder by mail and phone. Ask for pictures, lots of them, from the time he is a few weeks old until shortly before he is to come to you. When buying over the phone and from far away, it is best to deal with a reputable breeder, one who is well known for honesty and breeding ability. It's been told how prospective buyers get a photo of a selected puppy and, when the puppy arrives, it is not the same one as in the photo.

Ask what kind of guarantees come with the puppy. If the breeder says 30 days or less, forget about this breeder. No breeder can honestly give a buyer of a Bull Terrier puppy that kind of guarantee. Most problems do not manifest in just 30 days. Some problems do not appear until the dog has matured, some not even for five or six years.

MALE OR FEMALE?

Now that you have found a reputable breeder, you must decide on the very important question—a boy or a girl. If you are thinking on the idea of a girl, ask yourself these questions: 1) Do I wish to breed her? and 2) Am I in a position to raise a litter of puppies?

Choosing a male or female dog is a matter of preference, either sex will make a wonderful companion.

Not every female should be bred. Many Bull Terriers do not make good

mothers. The mildest of them can become little demons when it comes to raising a litter of babies. Some of the females have whelping problems. Many need to have cesarean births and require round-the-clock care. If you think you will have a litter to get back some of your purchase money, this may not happen. Litters can consist of between one to nine puppies. The average is five. In the litter of nine, you are fortunate to raise half of the litter.

Do you have time to raise a litter? The bitch needs supervision when whelping. You need to have the skills of a midwife to bring forth the whelps. Then, for the next 10 to 14 days, you need to be in attendance. You must keep a watchful eye on the dam so that she doesn't lie on or injure the babes. You must be sure that the pups are all nursing well. There are cases where the pups have had to be bottle fed for the first three weeks because Mom doesn't have any milk or her milk is bad.

Next comes the time to find your puppies good responsible homes. This requires a lot of time to meet many people. This all takes selective knowledge on your part.

He may be tiny now, but a Bull Terrier will attain most of his adult size by six months of age.

If you purchase a female that is not the highest quality to breed or show, have her spayed. This will not change her personality or make her fat. It will give you peace of mind that an accidental mating will not occur. It will also make for a cleaner, more sanitary pet.

Do you prefer to own a male? Not only are the males usually larger than the females, but it seems that the standard is describing a male. When you are all ready to take your macho dog for a stroll through the neighborhood, be ready for all kinds of inquiries, such as "Is that a Pit Bull?"

Male dogs do make very good house pets. They just need a bit different housetraining. It's natural for a male to be territorial and he will mark his boundaries. Unless a male dog is to be shown or used for stud, it is very important to have him neutered. This will add years to his life and spare him the agony of prostate cancer.

Bull Terriers come in a variety of colors. Seven-week-old "Gunner" is the perfect example of a black brindle puppy.

COLOR

Bull Terriers come in a variety of colors. Whites can have a patch of color on the head, near the eye, or on the ears. It seems that so many people want "one with an eye patch like Spuds'." The Whites also come "pure white" with no markings at all. When a White female is bred to a White male, it is impossible for the pups to be colored.

The Colored Bull Terrier comes in brindle, red, fawn, tricolored, black brindle, black and white, and black. Most colored dogs have white blazes, white chests, and white leg stockings. There are reds with black smut on the muzzle. Fawns can also carry this coloration. The tricolor is unique; the coloration is black, white, and tan. Some black brindles are confused with tricolored dogs because their brindling can be very light. The brindle will be on the legs and the sides of the head. Unless you have a desired color in mind, color should be of the least importance. Color has nothing to do with the make and shape of the dog. It does not effect the temperament.

Temperament testing will tell a lot about a pup's personality. A Bull Terrier puppy should seem interested and inquisitive about his surroundings.

Encourage your puppy to explore the world around him. New experiences will enrich his life and make him an active participant in his own socialization.

TEMPERAMENT

Temperament is the most important trait when selecting the puppy that will share your home and family. Look at the puppies as they play. Do not select the one that bites you or the other pups. This pup will probably need a lot of training in order not to be a bully later on. Leave this one for a more experienced owner.

Do not select the one that is cowering in the corner. He may be shy. He could be deaf or unilateral in hearing. Again, only a very wise and patient person should attempt to raise such a pup.

Just because the sire or dam is large does not mean that all of the pups will be large. There is no set size in the standard. Bull Terriers can be from 35 pounds to 70 pounds. In a litter, there are usually a variety of sizes. Do not hesitate to take the small one; he will usually catch up to his littermates. Also, smaller ones make better house pets for apartments and for the elderly.

This breed was designed for the maximum substance in the size. This is a big dog in a small package. You must have energy to cope with your puppy. A Bull Terrier puppy is full of playful energy. You will tire long before he will.

Now that we have explored all of the questions you may have, add one more thing to his menu. LOVE, LOVE, LOVE! He will return it to you a hundredfold.

CARING for Your Bull Terrier

FEEDING

When you first bring your puppy home, adhere to the breeder's list of do's and don'ts. Give strict attention to the diet that the puppy has already been following. This is a breed where the pup must eat good-quality nutritious food in order to grow. Some diets may call for milk, some may not. It depends upon the way the breeder has weaned the litter. A good diet may consist of puppy chow, cereals, meat, and dairy products, such as milk, cheese, cottage cheese, and yogurt.

Table scraps are safe if given in moderation. Nutritionally, table scraps supply calories, vitamins, and minerals. Avoid scraps such as fatty foods, chicken, or pork. Fatty foods, such as bacon grease, can cause diarrhea and digestive upsets. Poultry and pork bones are a definite no. They can lodge in the throat or intestinal tract, often with serious results that may lead to surgery. When adding table scraps to the food given, be sure that they make up no more than 10% of the meal. Treats from the table should never be given to the point that your pet avoids regular food.

Consult your breeder or veterinarian about the appropriate diet for your Bull Terrier.

Some Bull Terrier puppies become finicky eaters shortly after reaching their new home. Do not deter from the breeder's diet. Usually they will begin to eat when they get hungry enough. Do not start feeding the pup by hand or with a spoon. This can become a bad habit to break.

CRATES

After the pup has arrived home, you must decide where he will sleep. You can safely use a crate, such as an airline-style or metal-style crate. It really doesn't make any difference what type you use, as long it is comfortable and large enough for the pup to stand without touching the top of the crate with his head. A crate gives the pup a haven within the

Crates can be a dog's best friends. Aside from providing your Bull Terrier with a safe haven, they are also useful when traveling.

Your new puppy will look to you, his owner, to provide for all his needs.

house. It is a safe place to sleep and a safe place away from dangers such as electric cords, wall sockets, and plants. Any and all of these things can harm or kill your pet.

Do not let your new pup sleep with you on the bed. This can become a habit that is very hard to break. There is also a danger of the pup falling or jumping and breaking his leg. There are documented stories of the Bull Terrier puppy who, allowed to sleep in the bed, later becomes obsessive and will not allow his master in the bed. It has become his den. If roughly awakened, he can become dominant of his den or bed. So give him his own sleeping quarters from the start.

If you allow your Bull Terrier to develop bad habits, like lounging on your furniture, it can be very hard to break them.

Crates are also an excellent housebreaking tool. Your pup will not want to soil his bed. He will learn to hold himself until taken outside. When you travel in a car with your pet, he should be restrained for safety. You can place him in a crate and secure it with a seat belt or some bungee cords. There are also harness belts that fasten to the seat belt. In any case, he is quite safe and comfortable, and you can keep your eyes on the road. Also, the crate benefits the puppy and the other passengers. If car sickness occurs, he is in his crate, where a damp cloth will clean up the mess quickly. There will not be stains on the car seats.

A crate is also beneficial to the puppy that goes to dog shows. When at the dog shows, your Bull Terrier should be crated in the grooming area or in your van at ring side. Also, if flying with your dog, he must travel in a crate. So the early

Your Bull Terrier's crate should be made into a cozy den where he can relax. Line it with a soft blanket and provide him with toys to make him feel right at home.

crate training he receives as a puppy will benefit him later in life.

TRAVELING

A lot of owners like to travel in a car with their dog sitting on the front seat. Do not try this with an untrained dog. The Bull Terrier can eventually ride this way, but only after much training and maturity.

Your dog should never be allowed to travel in the back of an open pick-up truck. Not only is there the danger of him falling out of the truck, he might jump out. Also, the dog's eyes can be infected from dirt blowing up from the bed of the truck. If possible, use a truck cab. If you don't have one, please use a crate.

There may be times when you cannot take your Bull Terrier with you and you must board him instead. Before you take him to the nearest boarding kennel, do some homework. It is estimated that one in four pets visit a boarding facility at sometime during their life. Here's a check list to make your pet's stay a little more comfortable:

1. Are his vaccinations up to date? If not, have this done at least one week before his stay. It takes at least one week for immunity to develop. All boarding facilities handle a large number of pets. Thus, exposure to disease is a possibility.

2. Does the boarding kennel feed your brand of dog food? If not, be sure to take an ample supply of your dog's own food. Include his special treats and vitamins. If you let him eat the kennel's food, you may come back to a skinny dog. Bull Terriers do not like their food changed. If you cannot take enough of his food for the duration of his stay, at least take some that the kennel keeper can mix with the kennel food. Be sure you supply medications or special foods with clearly readable instructions.

3. Take any special blanket or toys. Remember you must try to make this stay as comfortable for him as possible.

4. Leave a number where you can be reached in case of

Be sure to provide your puppy with plenty of safe and healthy toys. Products made by Nylabone®, such as the Nylafloss™ and Frisbee™, are just the things!

If you decide to bring your Bull Terrier with you when you travel, bring along some familiar things, like his bed, to make him feel more at home.

an emergency. Also leave the number of the veterinarian or clinic that knows your dog and his medical history.

TOYS

When buying toys for the Bull Terrier, use extreme caution. Buy only Nylabone® toys such as rings, tugs, Frisbees™ or balls. When a toy becomes frayed at the edges, discard it. The Bull Terrier can bite off chunks and swallow them.

Do not buy soft plastic toys for the Bull Terrier. These will be eaten or pulled apart very easily. Tennis balls are to be used with caution. You can use a tennis ball in the show ring as baiting, but do not let the dog have it unattended. He can easily pop the ball, and the insides of the ball can be toxic. This is also true about the harder plastic toys that are covered with paintable surfaces. The lead in the paint is toxic. If your dog chews and swallows parts of this toy, he can become very ill or die from the paint.

Recently, a Bull Terrier chewed up a hard rubber ball manufactured by a famous supplier of dog items. When the owner of the dog called the breeder worried that the dog was

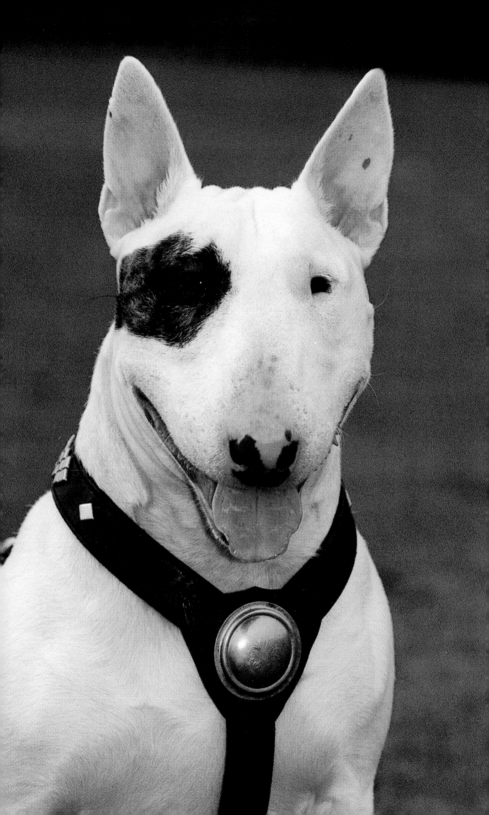

not eating, was vomiting, and had diarrhea, the breeder told her to get the dog to the vet immediately for x-rays. Sure enough, the x-ray showed a shadow in the stomach. After an emergency operation, the ball was taken out in pieces. Luckily, the ball was inside of the dog only two days. However, the lining of the intestinal wall was already showing signs of toxic poisoning. This was all done by a ball that you can find in any pet store or pet department.

HEALTH CONCERNS

Bull Terriers, as all purebred dogs, have some genetic health problems. For years, the breed has been plagued by deafness. A breeder usually did one of several things: 1) gave the pup away; 2) had it put to sleep; or 3) kept the pup himself. When the puppy did not respond to noise or the calling of his name, you realized the pup was deaf.

In 1992, the word "unilateral" crept into the Bull Terrier world. This is a condition where the dog hears from only one ear. It came to light when a top specialty winning Bull Terrier was found to be deaf at about two and one-half years of age. This dog had been extensively shown and gained his championship title under breeder judges. This concealment of the deafness was not done on purpose; the dog never showed any signs of deafness. When he was certified as deaf, it started a lot of concern among the breeders.

You'll surely fall in love with your Bull Terrier puppy. It is important to be aware of any particular health concerns.

A system called BAER testing was being done at the Veterinary School of Louisiana. Breeders set up testing clinics at the major shows across the country. Many of the top dogs were tested. The breeders were astonished at how many top breeding animals were affected by unilateral hearing.

Purchasing a Bull Terrier from a reputable breeder will ensure that your dog has a long and healthy life. Ywis Brindle Spot, owned by J. Bergman.

Even some Colored Bull Terriers were declared "unilateral." Up to that time, no

To ensure against genetic diseases, reputable breeders will screen all Bull Terriers before breeding them.

one ever heard of a Colored dog being deaf! Some of the breeders became obsessed to rid the Bull Terrier breed of any known dog with a hearing problem. Many breeders had their entire breeding stock spayed or neutered, whether they were afflicted or not, simply because they had a deaf relative somewhere in their lineage.

After much study, today's breeder is on the alert for the deaf factor. If you have a White bitch, with the deaf factor in her pedigree, she definitely should be bred only to a Colored male. The resulting puppies should be color bred when their turn comes for producing. This will help to lesson the ratio of deafness.

The story of a deaf Bull Terrier bitch comes from Juneau, Alaska. It seems that a young White Bull Terrier bitch was the companion of a sailor working on a fishing boat in the Alaskan waters. Coming ashore with him, somehow she lost him. She waited at the dock for each sailor and fisherman to board the ship. She sat and waited all night. At dawn the ship was ready to leave. Still, no sight of her master. She quietly sat on the dock watching the boat leave. No amount of coaxing could persuade her to go aboard. She was waiting for her special person. For about 12 years she met every ship that docked. She watched every fisherman or sailor that went on board but her friend never showed up. She was named "Patsy Ann" by the dock workers who fed and took care of her. She accepted their care, but would never leave her place on the docks. Finally, as old age crept into her life, she quietly went to sleep. Her waiting vigil was over.

Breeding Bull Terriers should only be undertaken by those with the knowledge and facilities to care for all of the puppies produced.

The miracle of this story is that Patsy Ann was deaf. She lived from 1929 to 1942. Most of her life was spent waiting for that one person she loved so much. The people of Juneau recently raised the money to have a bronze statue of Patsy Ann made by Anna Harris. The statue of Patsy Ann

sits in a little park by the information booth at the docks. She greets visitors from all over the world. It would have been nice if the breeders who rushed out and had their unilateral Bull Terriers spayed or neutered could have known Patsy Ann.

Bull Terriers also have several other genetic problems. Among them are luxating patella and kidney failure. In the past few years, reputable breeders have diligently bred away from carriers of these conditions.

Luxating patella is a bone condition of the back knee joints. The ball will slip out of the socket. This is a painful condition and causes the dog to be lame. It can be corrected with surgery, but the animal should not be used for breeding. Kidney failure is more serious. It will eventually lead to the death of the dog. There is no cure. Medication is available, but it is a long debilitating sickness.

One problem that gives a Bull Terrier a lot of agony is the flea. He simply cannot tolerate fleas. One flea and he is scratching himself raw. To keep him rid of fleas, use safe flea dips and sprays.

The Bull Terrier Club of America has a silent auction each year at the Silverwood Trophy Show. Items donated by members are auctioned to the highest bidder. This money is donated to research regarding the genetic conditions that befall the Bull Terrier. Not every Bull Terrier has a genetic problem. The majority lead full healthy lives. The low birth rate of the breed enables the breeders to get their puppies into selected homes. Here they will get proper home care and good veterinary medical care. Many Bull Terriers live up to 14 years and beyond. One is known to have celebrated his 18th birthday with no unusual sickness his whole life.

BREEDING YOUR BULL TERRIER

If one decides to breed his Bull Terrier, the owner of the bitch must be sure to mate her to the best compatible male to be found. A breeder should study pedigrees to find the right dog to compliment the bitch.

The breeder must decide whether to line breed or to outcross. Line breeding means the dog and the bitch will have common ancestors. Tight line breeding would be mating close relatives, such as half brother to half sister. An outcross is a mating of dogs not related at all.

Often in a breeding program, a breeder can be caught up in his own dogs and not see that he needs "a shot in the arm" in the form of an outside dog brought into the breeding program.

This excellent and adorable Bull Terrier puppy is a perfect example of good breeding.

Before deciding to breed any Bull Terrier, consider the make and shape of the dog. A dog must conform to the breed standard in order to be considered for breeding.

It is wise not to make a hasty trip to the top-winning dog of the moment. He may not be the right dog for your bitch. Breeding Bull Terriers takes a lot of study and good sense. It is an art to breed to produce champion after champion. You must use excellent breed specimens, both physically and temperamentally. The stud dog must carry several proponent qualities, such as a good, strong, typical head, broad with downface. He must have bone and substance. This does not mean size, but it means the maximum dog in the given space. He should be sound, even though the bitch is sound. This means he must have a reasonably good front, strong rear quarters, and he must move well with power and drive.

Make and Shape

Study the dog you are considering for stud from head to stern. Look at him sideways and front to back. Have him move for you. He should have good spring of rib, shortness of back,

The Hercules™ is made of very tough polyurethane. It is designed for Bull Terriers who are extremely strong chewers. The raised dental tips massage the gums and mechanically remove the plaque they encounter during chewing.

depth of brisket, and tuck-up of underline. All of these make up the dog's body shape.

If the bitch has a wrong bite but a good expression, you must use a stud with a good bite. Don't overlook a dog who has soft ears or a round eye; these are secondary faults. If your bitch is straight in stifle, you need to breed to a dog with well-bent stifles. When deciding on the right stud dog, first look for the proponent qualities and the best temperament. Next look at the secondary issues, such as ear and tail placement, nose, color, and coat.

Remember that your bitch should also be a good specimen, sound and of good temperament. She is 50% of the genetics of the future puppies.

Kennel-blind persons, inconsistent judges, and dog fanciers unfamiliar with Bull Terriers never develop a sense for assessing breed type. A knowledgeable breeder can take into account the virtues and faults and come up with a subjective appraisal of breed type. This ability is learned by experience and is usually a trait of the successful breeder.

Breed type changes and evolves over the years. It is generally a summation of the better breeding animals available at the time. A reigning stud dog will influence the breed for several years. Very seldom do you hear someone remark that the current winning show dog looks like the dam. It is usually said the show dog looks like the "dad."

Type varies in certain geographical areas; the dogs in England differ from those in America or South Africa or India. Certain faults will eliminate a Bull Terrier from being classed as typey, such as a poor dippy head or a tall weedy dog. It irritates the breeders sitting at ringside to see a shallow or weedy dog or a dog with a poor profile being given the blue ribbon at a dog show. They usually get very upset if a dog with obvious type gets completely passed over.

Dedicated Bull Terrier breeders all over the world work to improve the breed with each litter their kennels produce.

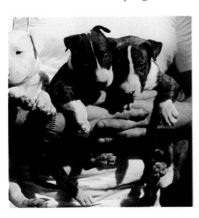

When exhibiting at all-breed shows, judges reward soundness over extreme breed virtues. This has resulted in many judges putting a sound Bull Terrier to a higher level of show records. This leaves the serious competing breeder or show exhibitor reluctant to exhibit at all-breed shows. Their dogs are shown at specialty shows that are presided over by breeder judges. The breeder judge will forgive a fault in favor of extreme virtues. This is a head breed, and no matter how we would like it to be different, the dog is judged by a breeder judge on his virtue of head. The faults are judged in degrees to the virtues, so it is not uncommon for a superior one with a mouth fault to go Best in Show. This dog would seldom win under the all-around judge.

Bull Terrier breeders around the world are working hard to improve the breed. Most breeders look beyond the dogs of today and imagine a time when all Bull Terriers will have beautiful heads with good bites, typey strong bodies, and sound movement. They know that the perfect dog will never exist. They do know that, in time, the general quality of Bull Terriers everywhere can be improved. This will be done by dedicated breeders working together.

Responsible breeders become upset when they hear of a litter produced by animals completely lacking breed type. The top breeders want to see all Bull Terriers (even "pet stock") demonstrate soundness and good breed type. Every time an unsound or poor-quality dog is used, it sets back the progress of breeding better Bull Terriers.

The Bull Terriers (as all purebred dogs) do have genetic defects. The question asked today is "What are we, as breeders, going to do about it?"

We can make an effort not to use dogs with a genetic defect. This is especially so when it comes to choosing a stud dog with luxating patellas, hearing impairment, kidney failure, heart disorders, and skin problems. The Bull Terrier gene pool consisting of those genes that produce blue eyes, high tail sets, flat feet, low-set ears, and most other faults that the breeder attempts to eliminate pose no major problems. The dog can still live a happy normal life. There are some deadly genes in the pool, but most are probably recessive.

Bull Terriers require some vegetable matter in their diet. The Carrot Bone™, made by Nylabone®, helps control plaque, eases the need to chew, and is nutritious. It is highly recommended as a healthy toy for your Bull Terrier.

Proper socialization when young will allow your Bull Terrier to get along with other dogs. "Spanky" and "Robin" give each other a warm greeting!

The best ways to eliminate faults is to breed animals that are as fault free as possible and to avoid doubling up on the same faults. Most breeders would like to avoid doubling up on defective genes or avoid introducing them into their breeding programs. This can only be done by knowing the pedigrees of the animals you use in your breeding program.

The Bull Terrier Club of America has established a committee to study hereditary problems in Bull Terriers. This Blue Ribbon Committee is made up of reputable breeders and it opened lines of communications among breeders. This committee was formed in 1987 and stayed in effect until 1994. The panel made great strides in its findings, which were released to the general Bull Terrier public. Although some health problems still exist, the panic on the part of the breeder has lessened. Breeders have the knowledge now to breed away from the genetic faults.

TRAINING Your Bull Terrier

The best training starts early. Some breeders suggest teaching the puppy at eight weeks to stand for examination. Place the puppy on a grooming table or other hard surface. Go over him with your hands. Place him in a standing position, feet placed as if showing. Run your hands lightly over his body. Examine his bite; take care not to hurt him. Do this each day until he accepts the touching and mouth examination without fussing. As he grows, you add other exercises. Do not overtire the puppy. Just a few minutes a day will suffice. Keep the exercises fun. You do not want him to get bored.

At about nine to ten weeks, begin to leash train him. Put a soft nylon collar on him, attach a small nylon leash, and let him drag it around the room. He will get used to it quickly. By the time he is ready to start training outdoors, he will be well acquainted with the leash. When starting, try to walk him outside. Tug the leash gently forward, urging him to "come." Use his name and repeat this exercise for a few days. Soon he will get the message that it is fun to walk along without pulling.

As the puppy grows and becomes more observant, start the basic obedience commands of sit, stay, and come. This can be

taught at home or at a puppy school. To teach him to sit, take your hand and gently push him into a sitting position. Hold him there for a few seconds. Let him up and start again. Each

Who knows how far a young puppy can go! Five-week-old "Indy" grew up to be a champion Bull Terrier.

Very basic training can begin at a relatively early age, once a puppy has been vaccinated and housebroken.

time use his name, tell him "sit," and praise him when he does it correctly. Even if he only sits a second, praise him. Do not reward him with a treat until the exercise is finished. Then give him a treat, telling him "good boy." When going to the commands stay or come, use the same basic rules. Show him what you want him to do. Be patient and reassuring. Praise him and give him a treat at the end of the exercise.

If you still have problems as your Bull Terrier gets older, such as getting into the garbage, chasing the mailman, pulling pillows off the sofa, or chewing things that do not belong to him, join an obedience club. This will take a lot of communication between you and your dog.

Many people think that the Bull Terrier is hard headed or stubborn. This so-called stubbornness is no more than the inherent nature of the dog, which at the moment of the problem is contrary to what the owner wants the dog to do. It will take excessive repetition to teach him what you wish him to learn, but the good news is he will learn it. Better still, what he learns, he will not forget. Therefore, you must be very careful what he learns.

Some Bull Terriers will excel in obedience, some will get through the course, and some will not. If you are asked to leave and not come back, this is usually because the dog has acted up. It may have frightened the other dog's owners, who have no idea what a Bull Terrier is. Also, many obedience trainers have never taught a Bull Terrier, let alone even seen one before.

If your puppy is very active, you may want to take him to kindergarten classes. The puppy is taught good manners, such as to not jump on people, to not run at high speed, and to not bark excessively. Puppy kindergarten will prepare him for the rigors of the big outside world and make him a happy positive Bull Terrier.

Never use harsh words with your dog. When you want him to obey, use a few clear, carefully chosen words. When you do not want him to do something, use the word "No." I have found the word "Don't" is effective also. The dog listens and stops whatever he is doing. Give the dog a few words that he associates with certain behaviors and make them memorable.

Bull Terriers are used today for therapy dogs. They visit nursing homes, children's centers, and schools. Many people believe that a Bull Terrier cannot swim but this is false. They can learn to swim and do like the water. They are not natural swimmers, but they will learn.

Bull Terriers are naturally outgoing and friendly, traits that make it easy for them to earn the Canine Good Citizen Certificate.

CANINE GOOD CITIZEN

In 1993, the Bull Terrier Club of America held its first Canine Good Citizen Trial Test at the Silverwood Weekend in Chicago. About 14 Bull Terriers registered for the event. They all finished and earned their Canine Good Citizen Certificate. These trials are held in conjunction with kennel club matches, fun matches, and just about anywhere a few dogs can gather. Mixed breeds can also take this test. At the Golden Triangle Bull Terrier Club's annual

The good-natured Bull Terrier is always up for some fun. This ballerina and her clown friend want to wish you a happy Halloween!

Although skateboarding isn't a part of basic trainig, these two buddies don't seem to mind the practice.

Well trained Bull Terriers can go anywhere! "Todd" demonstrates the importance of being properly trained on a ride in the park.

fun match in 1994, 11 Bull Terriers, one German Shepherd, three Schipperkes, one Golden Retriever and two mixed breeds took the test and all passed.

What is a Canine Good Citizen test? The program was designed in 1989 by AKC Secretary James Dearinger, partly in response to anti-canine sentiment. The program was intended to give pet owners a way to recognize the importance of having a well-behaved companion, and to show the public at large that dogs can be good citizens. The CGC is not a title of record and will not appear on official AKC papers. However, it may be included on unofficial pedigrees and in advertising.

Here is what a Canine Good Citizen must be able to do:

1. Canine Good Citizens should move confidently through crowds.

2. Canine Good Citizens should accept the friendly approaches of strangers.

3. Canine Good Citizens should sit down on command.

4. Canine Good Citizens should be able to pass by other dogs without disturbing them.

5. Canine Good Citizens should be able to walk through a crowd of people and sit patiently while others chat.

6. Canine Good Citizens must be able to be tied and be left alone for five minutes without wailing or excessive barking.

If your Bull Terrier can pass this test he will be welcomed anywhere!

BTCA RECOGNITION OF MERIT

In the late 1970s, Ralph Bowles and Robert (Bob) Thomas had some strong feelings about how many Bull Terriers were earning their AKC championships. Their idea was to identify the superior Bull Terriers that could advance the breed. The idea formed into the awarding of the Recognition of Merit (ROM) Championship by the BTCA. This title was awarded to Bull Terriers competing at the BTCA and regional club's specialties.

A healthy and tasty treat for your Bull Terrier because they love cheese is Chooz™. Chooz™ are bone-hard but can be microwaved to expand into a huge, crispy dog biscuit. They are almost fat free and about 70% protein.

At first it was conceived that the dogs could gain their title by winning at specialties. Points are awarded to the Best of Variety (BOV), Best of Opposite Sex (BOS), Winners Dog (WD), and Winners Bitch (WB). Dogs win with a three-point show, or two shows with two ROM points. At some point in the judging system that awards ROM points, a dog could win his ROM championship under one judge, but he needed seven total points. This system went through changes as the times dictated. As more regional clubs were formed, it was apparent there were more specialty shows, so the point system needed changing.

In 1989, the new point system changed. There was an increase in the total number of points required to earn the award, from seven to ten; an increase in the three-point award requirement, from one show to two; and the establishment of a minimum number of dogs that must be in competition in order for ROM points to be earned. In the past, the minimum number of dogs necessary to earn ROM points was based on the number of dogs to constitute an AKC major. This has been changed. There must now be at least six dogs of the same sex competing for Best of Variety and Best of Opposite Sex, and a total of five dogs of the same sex competing for Winners Dog and Winners Bitch. It was believed that these changes should improve the quality of the Bull Terriers that receive the ROM award and, in the process, improve the breed.

In the first 13 years, there were about ten ROM winners each year. From 1983 to 1988, there was an increase to an average of 25 ROM champions each year.

The BTCA Board became concerned that the award was given to too many Bull Terriers, so more changes were implanted. The ROM points were awarded to the BOV and BOS at the three-point shows, and two points to WD and WB (each variety). At the two-point shows, the BOV and BOS received two points each, and WD and WB got one point each. Also, a judge could award only one three-point ROM. Thus, a dog needed to win another three-point ROM under a different judge. The two point ROM could be awarded by the same judges.

This is how the judging stands today. But again, the system is being studied. There are still a great number of Bull Terriers winning the ROM championships. There are still a few dogs slipping into the ROM ranks that are not superior specimens of

There are all kinds of flying disks for dogs, but only one is made with strength, scent, and originality. The Nylabone® Frisbee™ is a must if you want to have this sort of fun with your Bull Terrier.

The trademark Frisbee is used under license from Mattel, Inc., California, USA.

the breed. These are highly competitive shows. Exhibitors often fly from coast to coast to win these points, especially the second three-point ROM. Many high-classed Bull Terriers never finish the ROM championship, as the dogs usually stay out in the ring past a certain age. They show for a year or more and rack up the unnecessary ROM points. This system severely limits a

Even if this Bull Terrier puppy is not of show quality, he'll still make a loving pet.

bitch's breeding time. There are those that have been campaigned until three or four years of age trying to earn that elusive three-point ROM. They lose to younger bitches. Bitches lose valuable breeding years because they are at their prime breeding from three to five years old.

Ralph Bowles is the Chairman of the ROM Awards committee. He tabulates the awards from the American Kennel Club Award catalog. The certificates are handed out at the yearly Silverwood banquet.

In 1979, Ch. Ann Dee's Red Adair, owned by Elaine Bernard, was the first Colored Bull Terrier to win the Silverwood Competition.

SPORT of Purebred Dogs

Welcome to the exciting and sometimes frustrating sport of dogs. No doubt you are trying to learn more about dogs or you wouldn't be deep into this book. This section covers the basics that may entice you, further your knowledge and help you to understand the dog world.

Dog showing has been a very popular sport for a long time and has been taken quite seriously by some. Others only enjoy it as a hobby.

All Bull Terriers, like four-and-one-half-month-old Abigail, can benefit from early training to teach them basic obedience and good manners.

The Kennel Club in England was formed in 1859, the American Kennel Club was established in 1884 and the Canadian Kennel Club was formed in 1888. The purpose of these clubs was to register purebred dogs and maintain their Stud Books. In the beginning, the concept of registering dogs was not

readily accepted. More than 36 million dogs have been enrolled in the AKC Stud Book since its inception in 1888. Presently the kennel clubs not only register dogs but adopt and enforce rules and regulations governing dog shows, obedience trials and field trials. Over the years they have fostered and encouraged interest in the health and welfare of the purebred dog. They routinely donate funds to veterinary research for study on genetic disorders.

With persistence, patience, and praise, your versatile Bull Terrier will become a well trained and obedient companion. Ch. Blackstone Benny, owned by Ann Dee.

Below are the addresses of the kennel clubs in the United States, Great Britain and Canada.

The American Kennel Club
51 Madison Avenue
New York, NY 10010
(Their registry is located at: 5580 Centerview Drive, STE 200, Raleigh, NC 27606-3390)

The Kennel Club
1 Clarges Street
Piccadilly, London, WIY 8AB, England

The Canadian Kennel Club
111 Eglinton Avenue
East Toronto, Ontario M6S 4V7
Canada

Today there are numerous activities that are enjoyable for both the dog and the handler. Some of the activities include conformation showing, obedience competition, tracking, agility, the Canine Good Citizen Certificate, and a wide range of instinct tests that vary from breed to breed. Where you start depends upon your goals which early on may not be readily apparent.

PUPPY KINDERGARTEN

Every puppy will benefit from this class. PKT is the foundation for all future dog activities from conformation to "couch potatoes." Pet owners should make an effort to attend even if they never expect to show their dog. The class is designed for puppies about three months of age with graduation at approximately five months of age. All the puppies will be in the same age group and, even though some may be a little unruly, there

This alert Bull Terrier eagerly awaits his owner's next command.

should not be any real problem. This class will teach the puppy some beginning obedience. As in all obedience classes the owner learns how to train his own dog. The PKT class gives the puppy the opportunity to interact with other puppies in the same age group and exposes him to strangers, which is very important. Some dogs grow up with behavior problems, one of them being fear of strangers. As you can see, there can be much to gain from this class.

There are some basic obedience exercises that every dog should learn. Some of these can be started with puppy kindergarten.

Sit

One way of teaching the sit is to have your dog on your left side with the leash in your right hand, close to the collar. Pull up on the leash and at the same time reach around his hindlegs with your left hand and tuck them in. As you are doing this say, "Beau, sit." Always use the dog's name when you give an active command. Some owners like to use a treat holding it over the dog's head. The dog will need to sit to get the treat. Encourage the dog to hold the sit for a few seconds, which will eventually be the beginning of the Sit/Stay. Depending on how cooperative he is, you can rub him under the chin or stroke his back. It is a good time to establish eye contact.

There are basic commands that every dog should know how to perform. "Axel" is learning how to heel.

Down

Sit the dog on your left side and kneel down beside him with the leash in your right hand. Reach over him with your left hand and grasp his left foreleg. With your right hand, take his right foreleg and pull his legs forward while you say, "Beau, down." If he tries to get up, lean on his shoulder to encourage him to stay down. It will relax your dog if you stroke his back while he is down. Try to encourage him to stay down for a few seconds as preparation for the Down/Stay.

Heel

The definition of heeling is the dog walking under control at your left heel. Your puppy will learn controlled walking in the puppy kindergarten class, which will eventually lead to heeling. The command is "Beau, heel," and you start off briskly with your left foot. Your leash is in your right hand and your left hand is holding it about half way down. Your left hand should be able to control the leash and there should be a little slack in it. You want him to walk with you with your leg somewhere between his nose and his shoulder. You need to encourage him to stay with you, not forging (in front of you) or lagging behind you. It is best to keep him on a fairly short lead. Do not allow the lead to become tight. It is far better to give him a little jerk when necessary and remind him to heel. When you come to a halt, be prepared physically to make him sit. It takes practice to become coordinated. There are excellent books on training that you may wish to purchase. Your instructor should be able to recommend one for you.

In conformation, your dog is judged by how closely he conforms to the breed standard. Am. Can. Ch. Lochiels Batteries Fire, ROM, owned by Sandra and Tom Frascone, shows us how it's done!

Recall

This quite possibly is the most important exercise you will ever teach. It should be a pleasant experience. The puppy may learn to do random recalls while being attached to a long line such as a clothes line. Later the exercise will start with the dog sitting and staying until called. The command is "Beau, come." Let your command be happy. You want your dog to come willingly and faithfully. The recall could save his life if he sneaks out the door. In practicing the recall, let him jump on you or touch you before you reach for him. If he is shy, then kneel down to his level. Reaching for the insecure dog could frighten him, and he may not be willing to come again in the future. Lots of praise and a treat would be in order whenever you do a recall. Under no circumstances should you ever correct your dog when he has come to you. Later in formal obedience your dog will be required to sit in front of you after recalling and then go to heel position.

CONFORMATION

Conformation showing is our oldest dog show sport. This type of showing is based on the dog's appearance—that is his structure, movement and attitude. When considering this type of showing, you need to be aware of your breed's standard and be able to evaluate your dog compared to that standard. The breeder of your puppy or other experienced breeders would be good sources for such an evaluation. Puppies can go through lots of changes over a period of time. Many puppies start out as promising hopefuls and then after maturing may be disappointing as show candidates. Even so this should not deter them from being excellent pets.

Usually conformation training classes are offered by the local kennel or obedience clubs. These are excellent places for training puppies. The puppy should be able to walk on a lead before entering such a class. Proper ring procedure and technique for posing (stacking) the dog will be demonstrated as well as gaiting the dog. Usually certain patterns are used in the ring such as the triangle or the "L." Conformation class, like the PKT class, will give your youngster the opportunity to socialize with different breeds of dogs and humans too.

Hand signals in conjunction with verbal commands can be helpful in training your Bull Terrier. Ch. Headstrong Heritage.

Puppy kindergarten is not only a good way to teach basic obedience commands, but it also allows invaluable opportunity for socialization.

It takes some time to learn the routine of conformation showing. Usually one starts at the puppy matches that may be AKC Sanctioned or Fun Matches. These matches are generally for puppies from two or three months to a year old, and there may be classes for the adult over the age of 12 months. Similar to point shows, the classes are divided by sex and after completion of the classes in that breed or variety, the class winners compete for Best of Breed or Variety. The winner goes on to compete in the Group and the Group winners compete for Best in Match. No championship points are awarded for match wins.

A few matches can be great training for puppies even though there is no intention to go on showing. Matches enable the puppy to meet new people and be handled by a stranger—the judge. It is also a change of environment, which broadens the horizon for both dog and handler. Matches and other dog activities boost the confidence of the handler and especially the younger handlers.

Earning an AKC championship is built on a point system, which is different from Great Britain. To become an AKC Champion of Record the dog must earn 15 points. The number of points earned each time depends upon the number of dogs in competition. The number of points available at each show depends upon the breed, its sex and the location of the show. The United States is divided into ten AKC zones. Each zone has its own set of points. The purpose of the zones is to try to equalize the points available from breed to breed and area to area. The AKC adjusts the point scale annually.

The number of points that can be won at a show are between one and five. Three-, four- and five-point wins are considered majors. Not only does the dog need 15 points won under three different judges, but those points must include two majors under two different judges. Canada also works on a point system but majors are not required.

Dogs always show before bitches. The classes available to those seeking points are: Puppy (which may be divided into 6 to 9 months and 9 to 12 months); 12 to 18 months; Novice; Bred-by-Exhibitor; American-bred; and Open. The class winners of the same sex of each breed or variety compete against each other for Winners Dog and Winners Bitch. A Reserve Winners Dog and Reserve Winners Bitch are also awarded but do not carry any points unless the Winners win is

Conformation training classes are often offered by local kennels and obedience clubs. Ch. Bullyrook Inxs demonstrates his stance.

disallowed by AKC. The Winners Dog and Bitch compete with the specials (those dogs that have attained championship) for Best of Breed or Variety, Best of Winners and Best of Opposite Sex. It is possible to pick up an extra point or even a major if the points are higher for the defeated winner than those of Best of Winners. The latter would get the higher total from the defeated winner.

Remember, every hardworking Bull Terrier needs a break sometimes! This guy takes a well-deserved rest.

At an all-breed show, each Best of Breed or Variety winner will go on to his respective Group and then the Group winners will compete against each other for Best in Show. There are seven Groups: Sporting, Hounds, Working, Terriers, Toys, Non-Sporting and Herding. Obviously there are no Groups at speciality shows (those shows that have only one breed or a show such as the American Spaniel Club's Flushing Spaniel Show, which is for all flushing spaniel breeds).

Successful showing requires dedication and preparation, but most of all, it should be an enjoyable experience for handlers and dogs alike.

Earning a championship in England is somewhat different since they do not have a point system. Challenge Certificates are awarded if the judge feels the dog is deserving regardless of the number of dogs in competition. A dog must earn three Challenge Certificates under three different judges, with at least one of these Certificates being won after the age of 12 months. Competition is very strong and entries may be higher than they are in the U.S. The Kennel Club's Challenge Certificates are only available at Championship Shows.

In England, The Kennel Club regulations require that certain dogs, Border Collies and Gundog breeds, qualify in a working capacity (i.e., obedience or field trials) before becoming a full Champion. If they do not qualify in the working aspect, then they are designated a Show Champion, which is equivalent to the AKC's Champion of Record. A Gundog may be granted the title of Field Trial Champion (FT Ch.) if it passes all the tests in the field but would also have to qualify in conformation before becoming a full Champion. A Border Collie that

Every Bull Terrier is a champion in his owner's eyes, and these two friends are sure of it!

earns the title of Obedience Champion (Ob Ch.) must also qualify in the conformation ring before becoming a Champion.

The U.S. doesn't have a designation full Champion but does award for Dual and Triple Champions. The Dual Champion must be a Champion of Record, and either Champion Tracker, Herding Champion, Obedience Trial Champion or Field Champion. Any dog that has been awarded the titles of Champion of Record, and any two of the following: Champion Tracker, Herding Champion, Obedience Trial Champion or Field Champion, may be designated as a Triple Champion.

The shows in England seem to put more emphasis on breeder judges than those in the U.S. There is much competition within the breeds. Therefore the quality of the individual breeds should be very good. In the United States we tend to have more "all around judges" (those that judge multiple breeds) and use the breeder judges at the specialty shows. Breeder judges are more familiar with their own breed since they are actively breeding

Dogs are a very important part of their owner's lives, and the bond between humans and animals is a strong one.

that breed or did so at one time. Americans emphasize Group and Best in Show wins and promote them accordingly.

The shows in England can be very large and extend over several days, with the Groups being scheduled on different days. Though multi-day shows are not common in the U.S., there are cluster shows, where several different clubs will use the same show site over consecutive days.

Westminster Kennel Club is our most prestigious show although the entry is limited to 2500. In recent years, entry has been limited to Champions. This show is more formal than the majority of the shows with the judges wearing formal attire and the handlers fashionably dressed. In most instances the quality of the dogs is superb. After all, it is a show of Champions. It is a good show to study the AKC registered breeds and is by far the most exciting—especially since it is televised! WKC is one of the few shows in this country that is still benched. This means the dog must be in his benched area during the show hours except when he is being groomed, in the ring, or being exercised.

Typically, the handlers are very particular about their appearances. They are careful not to wear something that will detract from their dog but will perhaps enhance it. American ring procedure is quite formal compared to that of other countries. There is a certain etiquette expected between the judge and exhibitor and among the other exhibitors. Of course it is not always the case but the judge is supposed to be polite, not engaging in small talk or acknowledging how well he knows the handler. There is a more informal and relaxed atmosphere at the shows in other countries. For instance, the dress code is more casual. I can see where this might be more fun for the exhibitor and especially for the novice. The U.S. is very handler-oriented in many of the breeds. It is true, in most instances, that the experienced professional handler can present the dog better and will have a feel for what a judge likes.

Ch. Ann Dees Smokin Joe, ROM, owned by Betty Desmond, Elaine Bernard, and Sandra Frascone, has been a Specialty Winner and Silverwood Finalist.

In England, Crufts is The Kennel Club's own show and is most assuredly the largest dog show in the world. They've been known to have an entry of nearly 20,000, and the show lasts four days. Entry is only gained by qualifying through winning in specified classes at another Championship Show. Westminster is strictly conformation, but Crufts exhibitors and spectators enjoy not only conformation but obedience, agility and a multitude of exhibitions as well. Obedience was admitted in 1957 and agility in 1983.

If you are handling your own dog, please give some consideration to your apparel. For sure the dress code at matches is more informal than the point shows. However, you should wear something a little more appropriate than beach attire or ragged jeans and bare feet. If you check out the handlers and see what is presently fashionable, you'll catch on. Men usually dress with a shirt and tie and a nice sports coat. Whether you are male or female, you will want to wear comfortable clothes and shoes. You need to be able to run with your dog and you certainly don't want to take a chance of

BEST OF
BREED/VARIETY

TRINITY VALLEY
KENNEL CLUB

MARCH 1993

© NUGENT PHOTO

falling and hurting yourself. Heaven forbid, if nothing else, you'll upset your dog. Women usually wear a dress or two-piece outfit, preferably with pockets to carry bait, comb, brush, etc. In this case men are the lucky ones with all their pockets. Ladies, think about where your dress will be if you need to kneel on the floor and also think about running. Does it allow freedom to do so?

With the proper training and attention, your Bull Terrier puppy can become all that you want him to be—the perfect pet companion.

You need to take along dog; crate; ex pen (if you use one); extra newspaper; water pail and water; all required grooming equipment, including hair dryer and extension cord; table; chair for you; bait for dog and lunch for you and friends; and, last but not least, clean up materials, such as plastic bags, paper towels, and perhaps a bath towel and some shampoo— just in case. Don't forget your entry confirmation and directions to the show.

If you are showing in obedience, then you will want to wear pants. Many of our top obedience handlers wear pants that are color-coordinated with their dogs. The philosophy is that imperfections in the black dog will be less obvious next to your black pants.

Whether you are showing in conformation, Junior Showmanship or obedience, you need to watch the clock and be sure you are not late. It is customary to pick up your

Ch. Ann Dee's Crimson Tide, owned by Jim Arrington, winning Best of Variety.

conformation armband a few minutes before the start of the class. They will not wait for you and if you are on the show grounds and not in the ring, you will upset everyone. It's a little more complicated picking up your obedience armband if you show later in the class. If you have not picked up your armband and they get to your number, you may not be allowed to show. It's best to pick up your armband early, but then you may show earlier than expected if other handlers don't pick up. Customarily all conflicts should be discussed with the judge prior to the start of the class.

Junior Showmanship

The Junior Showmanship Class is a wonderful way to build self confidence even if there are no aspirations of staying with the dog-show game later in life. Frequently, Junior Showmanship becomes the background of those who become successful exhibitors/handlers in the future. In some instances it is taken very seriously, and success is measured in terms of wins. The Junior Handler is judged solely on his ability and skill in presenting his dog. The dog's conformation is not to be considered by the judge. Even so the condition and grooming of the dog may be a reflection upon the handler.

Usually the matches and point shows include different classes. The Junior Handler's dog may be entered in a breed or obedience class and even shown by another person in that class. Junior Showmanship classes are usually divided by age and perhaps sex. The age is determined by the handler's age on the day of the show. The classes are:

Novice Junior for those at least ten and under 14 years of age who at time of entry closing have not won three first places in a Novice Class at a licensed or member show.

Novice Senior for those at least 14 and under 18 years of age who at the time of entry closing have not won three first places in a Novice Class at a licensed or member show.

Open Junior for those at least ten and under 14 years of age who at the time of entry closing have won at least three first places in a Novice Junior Showmanship Class at a licensed or member show with competition present.

Open Senior for those at least 14 and under 18 years of age who at time of entry closing have won at least three first places in a Novice Junior Showmanship Class at a licensed or member show with competition present.

Junior Handlers must include their AKC Junior Handler number on each show entry. This needs to be obtained from the AKC.

CANINE GOOD CITIZEN

The AKC sponsors a program to encourage dog owners to train their dogs. Local clubs perform the pass/fail tests, and dogs who pass are awarded a Canine Good Citizen Certificate. Proof of vaccination is required at the time of participation. The test includes:

1. Accepting a friendly stranger.
2. Sitting politely for petting.
3. Appearance and grooming.
4. Walking on a loose leash.
5. Walking through a crowd.
6. Sit and down on command/staying in place.
7. Come when called.
8. Reaction to another dog.

9. Reactions to distractions.
10. Supervised separation.

If more effort was made by pet owners to accomplish these exercises, fewer dogs would be cast off to the humane shelter.

OBEDIENCE

Obedience is necessary, without a doubt, but it can also become a wonderful hobby or even an obsession. Obedience classes and competition can provide wonderful companionship, not only with your dog but with your classmates or fellow competitors. It is always gratifying to discuss your dog's problems with others who have had similar experiences. The AKC acknowledged Obedience around 1936, and it has changed tremendously even though many of the exercises are basically the same. Today, obedience competition is just that—very competitive. Even so, it is possible for every obedience exhibitor to come home a winner (by earning qualifying scores) even though he/she may not earn a placement in the class.

Canine Good Citizens must be able to get along with all kinds of people, including children. This Bull Terrier pup looks like he's getting an early start.

Most of the obedience titles are awarded after earning three qualifying scores (legs) in the appropriate class under three different judges. These classes offer a perfect score of 200, which is extremely rare. Each of the class exercises has its own point value. A leg is earned after receiving a score of at least 170 and at least 50 percent of the points available in each exercise. The titles are:

Companion Dog—CD
This is called the Novice Class and the exercises are:

1.Heel on leash and figure 8	40 points
2.Stand for examination	30 points
3.Heel free	40 points
4.Recall	30 points
5.Long sit—one minute	30 points
6.Long down—three minutes	30 points
Maximum total score	200 points

Companion Dog Excellent—CDX
This is the Open Class and the exercises are:

1.Heel off leash and figure 8	40 points
2.Drop on recall	30 points
3.Retrieve on flat	20 points
4.Retrieve over high jump	30 points
5.Broad jump	20 points
6.Long sit—three minutes (out of sight)	30 points
7.Long down—five minutes (out of sight)	30 points
Maximum total score	200 points

Utility Dog—UD
The Utility Class exercises are:

1.Signal Exercise	40 points
2.Scent discrimination-Article 1	30 points
3.Scent discrimination-Article 2	30 points
4.Directed retrieve	30 points
5.Moving stand and examination	30 points
6.Directed jumping	40 points
Maximum total score	200 points

After achieving the UD title, you may feel inclined to go after the UDX and/or OTCh. The UDX (Utility Dog Excellent) title went into effect in January 1994. It is not easily attained.

The title requires qualifying simultaneously ten times in Open B and Utility B but not necessarily at consecutive shows.

The OTCh (Obedience Trial Champion) is awarded after the dog has earned his UD and then goes on to earn 100 championship points, a first place in Utility, a first place in Open and another first place in either class. The placements must be won under three different judges at all-breed obedience trials. The points are determined by the number of dogs competing in the Open B and Utility B classes. The OTCh title precedes the dog's name.

Obedience matches (AKC Sanctioned, Fun, and Show and Go) are usually available. Usually they are sponsored by the local obedience clubs. When preparing an obedience dog for a title, you will find matches very helpful. Fun Matches and Show and Go Matches are more lenient in allowing you to make corrections in the ring. This type of training is usually very necessary for the Open and Utility Classes. AKC Sanctioned Obedience Matches do not allow corrections in the ring since they must abide by the AKC Obedience Regulations.

Agility competition is growing in popularity. Tessi, owned by Dorinda Desment, easily clears the bar jump.

If you are interested in showing in obedience, then you should contact the AKC for a copy of the Obedience Regulations.

The Bull Terrier is an energetic and intelligent dog and will be most happy when active.

TRACKING

Tracking is officially classified obedience. There are three tracking titles available: Tracking Dog (TD), Tracking Dog Excellent (TDX), Variable Surface Tracking (VST). If all three tracking titles are obtained, then the dog officially becomes a CT (Champion Tracker). The CT will go in front of the dog's name.

A TD may be earned anytime and does not have to follow the other obedience titles. There are many exhibitors that prefer tracking to obedience, and there are others who do both.

Tracking Dog–TD

A dog must be certified by an AKC tracking judge that he is ready to perform in an AKC test. The AKC can provide the names of tracking judges in your area that you can contact for certification. Depending on where you live, you may have to travel a distance if there is no local tracking judge. The certification track will be equivalent to a regular AKC track. A regulation track must be 440 to 500 yards long with at least two right-angle turns out in the open. The track will be aged 30 minutes to two hours. The handler has two starting flags at the beginning of the track to indicate the direction started. The dog works on a harness and 40-foot lead and must work at least 20 feet in front of the handler. An article (either a dark glove or wallet) will be dropped at the end of the track, and the dog must indicate it but not necessarily retrieve it.

Agility tests like the tire jump allow the Bull Terrier to apply his natural abilities to the competition ring.

People always ask what the dog tracks. Initially, the beginner on the short-aged track tracks the tracklayer. Eventually the dog learns to track the disturbed vegetation and learns to differentiate between tracks. Getting started with tracking requires reading the AKC regulations and a good book on tracking plus finding other tracking enthusiasts. Work on the buddy system. That is—lay tracks for each other so you can practice blind tracks. It is possible to train on your own, but if you are a beginner, it is a lot more entertaining to track with a buddy. It's rewarding seeing the dog use his natural ability.

AGILITY

Agility was first introduced by John Varley in England at the Crufts Dog Show, February 1978, but Peter Meanwell, competitor and judge, actually developed the idea. It was officially recognized in the early '80s. Agility is extremely popular in England and Canada and growing in popularity in the U.S. The AKC acknowledged agility in August 1994. Dogs must be at least 12 months of age to be entered. It is a fascinating sport that the dog, handler and spectators enjoy to the utmost. Agility is a spectator sport! The dog performs off lead. The handler either runs with his dog or positions himself on the course and directs his dog with verbal and hand signals over a timed course over or through a variety of obstacles including a time out or pause. One of the main drawbacks to agility is finding a place to train. The obstacles take up a lot of space and it is very time consuming to put up and take down courses.

The titles earned at AKC agility trials are Novice Agility Dog (NAD), Open Agility Dog (OAD), Agility Dog Excellent (ADX), and Master Agility Excellent (MAX). In order to acquire *The playful Bull Terrier needs regular activity and will enjoy a romp in the yard.* an agility title, a dog must earn a qualifying score in its respective class on three separate occasions under two different judges. The MAX will be awarded after earning ten qualifying scores in the Agility Excellent Class.

PERFORMANCE TESTS

During the last decade the American Kennel Club has promoted performance tests—those events that test the different breeds' natural abilities. This type of event encourages a handler to devote even more time to his dog and retain the natural instincts of his breed heritage. It is an important part of the wonderful world of dogs.

Earthdog Events

For small terriers (Australian, Bedlington, Border, Cairn, Dandie Dinmont, Fox (Smooth & Wire), Lakeland, Norfolk, Norwich, Scottish, Sealyham, Skye, Welsh, West Highland White and Dachshunds).

Limited registration (ILP) dogs are eligible and all entrants must be at least six months

Training for any type of competition allows the owner and his dog to develop closeness through working together.

of age. The primary purpose of the small terriers and Dachshunds is to pursue quarry to ground, hold the game, and alert the hunter where to dig, or to bolt. There are two parts to the test: (1) the approach to the quarry and (2) working the quarry. The dog must pass both parts for a Junior Earthdog (JE). The Senior Earthdog (SE) must do a third part—to leave the den on command. The Master Earthdog (ME) is a bit more complicated.

GENERAL INFORMATION

Obedience, tracking and agility allow the purebred dog with an Indefinite Listing Privilege (ILP) number or a limited registration to be exhibited and earn titles. Application must be made to the AKC for an ILP number.

The American Kennel Club publishes a monthly *Events* magazine that is part of the *Gazette*, their official journal for the sport of purebred dogs. The *Events* section lists upcoming shows and the secretary or superintendent for them. The majority of the conformation shows in the U.S. are overseen by licensed superintendents. Generally the entry closing date is approximately two-and-a-half weeks before the actual show. Point shows are fairly expensive, while the match shows cost about one third of the point show entry fee. Match shows usually take entries the day of the show but some are pre-entry. The best way to find match show information is through your local kennel club. Upon asking, the AKC can provide you with a list of superintendents, and you can write and ask to be put on their mailing lists.

Obedience trial and tracking test information is available

Derick is a typical Bull Terrier pup— he just wants to get out and play!

through the AKC. Frequently these events are not superintended, but put on by the host club. Therefore you would make the entry with the event's secretary.

As you have read, there are numerous activities you can share with your dog. Regardless what you

There are so many activities that your dog can participate in, and the versatile Bull Terrier has the ability to excel at them all!

Agility is just one of the many activities in which the Bull Terrier can demonstrate his athletic and competitive prowess.

do, it does take teamwork. Your dog can only benefit from your attention and training. We hope this chapter has enlightened you and hope, if nothing else, you will attend a show here and there. Perhaps you will start with a puppy kindergarten class, and who knows where it may lead!

HEALTH CARE

Veterinary medicine has become far more sophisticated than what was available to our ancestors. This can be attributed to the increase in household pets and consequently the demand for better care for them. Also human medicine has become far more complex. Today diagnostic testing in veterinary medicine parallels human diagnostics. Because of better technology we can expect our pets to live healthier lives thereby increasing their life spans.

THE FIRST CHECK UP

You will want to take your new puppy/dog in for its first check up within 48 to 72 hours after acquiring it. Many breeders strongly recommend this check up and so do the humane shelters. A puppy/dog can appear healthy but it may have a serious problem that is not apparent to the layman. Most pets have some type of a minor flaw that may never cause a real problem.

For the sake of your puppy as well as the health of your family, you should bring your new Bull Terrier to the veterinarian within three days of his arrival at your home.

Through breeding dogs that are only of the best quality we are assured that good health and temperament will be passed down to each new generation.

Unfortunately if he/she should have a serious problem, you will want to consider the consequences of keeping the pet and the attachments that will be formed, which may be broken prematurely. Keep in mind there are many healthy dogs looking for good homes.

This first check up is a good time to establish yourself with the veterinarian and learn the office policy regarding their hours and how they handle emergencies. Usually the breeder or another conscientious pet owner is a good reference for locating a capable veterinarian. You should be aware that not all veterinarians give the same quality of service. Please do not make your selection on the least expensive clinic, as they may be short changing your pet. There is the possibility that eventually it will cost you more due to improper diagnosis, treatment, etc. If you are selecting a new veterinarian, feel free to ask for a tour of the clinic. You should inquire about making an appointment for a tour since all clinics are working clinics, and therefore may not be available all day for sightseers. You may worry less if you see where your pet will be spending the day if he ever needs to be hospitalized.

THE PHYSICAL EXAM

Your veterinarian will check your pet's overall condition, which includes listening to the heart; checking the respiration; feeling the abdomen, muscles and joints; checking the mouth, which includes the gum color and signs of gum disease along with plaque buildup; checking the ears for signs of an infection or ear mites; examining the eyes; and, last but not least, checking the condition of the skin and coat.

He should ask you questions regarding your pet's eating and elimination habits and invite you to relay your questions. It is a good idea to prepare a list so as not to forget anything. He should discuss the proper diet and the quantity to be fed. If this should differ from your breeder's recommendation, then you should convey to him the breeder's choice and see if he approves. If he recommends changing the diet, then this should be done over a few days so as not to cause a gastrointestinal upset. It is customary to take in a fresh stool sample (just a small amount) for a test for intestinal parasites. It must be fresh, preferably within 12 hours, since the eggs hatch quickly and after hatching will not be observed under the microscope. If your pet isn't obliging then, usually the technician can take one in the clinic.

POPpup's® are healthy treats for your Bull Terrier. When bone-hard they help to control plaque build-up; when microwaved they become a rich cracker, which your Bull Terrier will love. The POPpup® is available in liver and other flavors and is fortified with calcium.

IMMUNIZATIONS

It is important that you take your puppy/dog's vaccination record with you on your first visit. In the case of a puppy, presumably the breeder has seen to the vaccinations up to the time you acquired custody. Veterinarians differ in their vaccination protocol. It is not unusual for

Regular medical care is just as important for the adult Bull Terrier as it is for the puppy.

Vaccinations are extremely important to your puppy's health. Be sure that your veterinarian is provided with records of the immunizations your puppy has already received.

your puppy to have received vaccinations for distemper, hepatitis, leptospirosis, parvovirus and parainfluenza every two to three weeks from the age of five or six weeks. Usually this is a combined injection and is typically called the DHLPP. The DHLPP is given through at least 12 to 14 weeks of age, and it is customary to

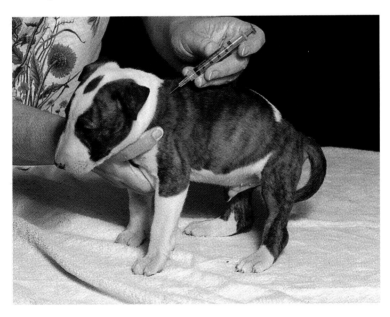

continue with another parvovirus vaccine at 16 to 18 weeks. You may wonder why so many immunizations are necessary. No one knows for sure when the puppy's maternal antibodies are gone, although it is customarily accepted that distemper antibodies are gone by 12 weeks. Usually parvovirus antibodies are gone by 16 to 18 weeks of age. However, it is possible for the maternal antibodies to be gone at a much earlier age or even a later age. Therefore immunizations are started at an early age. The vaccine will not give immunity as long as there are maternal antibodies.

The rabies vaccination is given at three or six months of age depending on your local laws. A vaccine for bordetella (kennel cough) is advisable and can be given anytime from the age of five weeks. The coronavirus is not commonly given unless there is a problem locally. The Lyme vaccine is necessary in endemic areas. Lyme disease has been reported in 47 states.

Distemper

This is virtually an incurable disease. If the dog recovers, he is subject to severe nervous disorders. The virus attacks every tissue in the body and resembles a bad cold with a fever. It can cause a runny nose and eyes and cause gastrointestinal disorders, including a poor appetite, vomiting and diarrhea. The virus is carried by raccoons, foxes, wolves, mink and other dogs. Unvaccinated youngsters and senior citizens are very susceptible. This is still a common disease.

Hepatitis

This is a virus that is most serious in very young dogs. It is spread by contact with an infected animal or its stool or urine. The virus affects the liver and kidneys and is characterized by high fever, depression and lack of appetite. Recovered animals may be afflicted with chronic illnesses.

Leptospirosis

This is a bacterial disease transmitted by contact with the urine of an infected dog, rat or other wildlife. It produces severe symptoms of fever, depression, jaundice and internal bleeding and was fatal before the vaccine was developed. Recovered dogs can be carriers, and the disease can be transmitted from dogs to humans.

Parvovirus

This was first noted in the late 1970s and is still a fatal disease. However, with proper vaccinations, early diagnosis and prompt treatment, it is a manageable disease. It attacks the bone marrow and intestinal tract. The symptoms include depression, loss of appetite, vomiting, diarrhea and collapse. Immediate medical attention is of the essence.

Bordetella attached to canine cilia. Otherwise known as kennel cough, this disease is highly contagious and should be vaccinated against routinely.

Rabies

This is shed in the saliva and is carried by raccoons, skunks, foxes, other dogs and cats. It attacks nerve tissue, resulting in paralysis and death. Rabies can be transmitted to people and is virtually always fatal. This disease is reappearing in the suburbs.

Bordetella (Kennel Cough)

The symptoms are coughing, sneezing, hacking and retching accompanied by nasal discharge usually lasting from a few days to several weeks. There are several disease-producing organisms responsible for this disease. The present vaccines are helpful but do not protect for all the strains. It usually is not life threatening but in some instances it can progress to a

serious bronchopneumonia. The disease is highly contagious. The vaccination should be given routinely for dogs that come in contact with other dogs, such as through boarding, training class or visits to the groomer.

Coronavirus

This is usually self limiting and not life threatening. It was first noted in the late '70s about a year before parvovirus. The

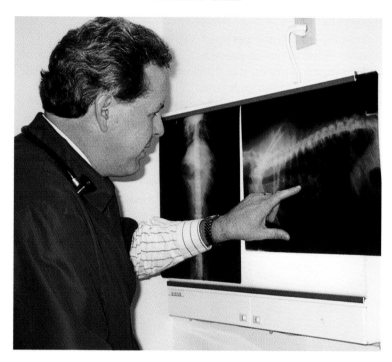

Regular visits to the veterinarian will help in the timely diagnosis of any illnesses or parasitic infections.

virus produces a yellow/ brown stool and there may be depression, vomiting and diarrhea.

Lyme Disease

This was first diagnosed in the United States in 1976 in Lyme, CT in people who lived in close proximity to the deer tick. Symptoms may include acute lameness, fever, swelling of joints and loss of appetite. Your veterinarian can advise you if you live in an endemic area.

After your puppy has completed his puppy vaccinations, you will continue to booster the DHLPP once a year. It is customary to booster the rabies one year after the first vaccine and then, depending on where you live, it should be boostered every year or every three years. This depends on your local laws. The Lyme and corona vaccines are boostered annually and it is recommended that the bordetella be boostered every six to eight months.

Annual Visit

I would like to impress the importance of the annual check up, which would include the booster vaccinations, check for intestinal parasites and test for heartworm. Today in our very busy world it is rush, rush and see "how much you can get for how little." Unbelievably, some non-veterinary businesses have entered into the vaccination business. More harm than good can come to your dog through improper vaccinations, possibly from inferior vaccines and/or the wrong schedule. More than likely you truly care about your companion dog and over the years you have devoted much time and expense to his well being. Perhaps you are unaware that a vaccination is not just a vaccination. There is more involved. Please, please follow through with regular physical examinations. It is so important for your veterinarian to know your dog and this is especially true during middle age through the geriatric years. More than likely your older dog will require more than one physical a year. The annual physical is good preventive medicine. Through early diagnosis and subsequent treatment your dog can maintain a longer and better quality of life.

The deer tick is the most common carrier of Lyme disease. Photo courtesy of Virbac Laboratories, Inc., Fort Worth, Texas.

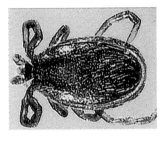

Intestinal Parasites

Hookworms

These are almost microscopic intestinal worms that can cause anemia and therefore serious problems, including death, in young puppies. Hookworms can be transmitted to humans through penetration of the skin. Puppies may be born with them.

Roundworms

These are spaghetti-like worms that can cause a potbellied appearance and dull coat along with more severe symptoms, such as vomiting, diarrhea and coughing. Puppies acquire these while in the mother's uterus and through lactation. Both hookworms and roundworms may be acquired through ingestion.

Whipworms

These have a three-month life cycle and are not acquired through the dam. They cause intermittent diarrhea usually with mucus. Whipworms are possibly the most difficult worm to eradicate. Their eggs are very resistant to most environmental factors and can last for years until the proper conditions enable them to mature. Whipworms are seldom seen in the stool.

Intestinal parasites are more prevalent in some areas than others. Climate, soil and contamination are big factors contributing to the incidence of intestinal parasites. Eggs are passed in the stool, lay on the ground and then become infective in a certain number of days. Each of the above worms has a different life cycle. Your best chance of becoming and remaining worm-free is to always pooper-scoop your yard. A fenced-in yard keeps stray dogs out, which is certainly helpful.

I would recommend having a fecal examination on your dog twice a year or more often if there is a problem. If your dog has a positive fecal sample, then he will be given the appropriate medication and you will be asked to bring back another stool sample in a certain period of time (depending on the type of worm) and then be rewormed. This process goes on until he has at least two negative samples. The different types of worms require different medications. You will be wasting your money and doing your dog an injustice by buying over-the-counter medication without first consulting your veterinarian.

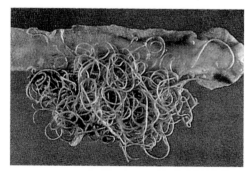

When visiting the veterinarian, it is customary to take a stool sample to test for intestinal parasites, such as roundworms. Courtesy of Merck AgVet.

Other Internal Parasites

Coccidiosis and Giardiasis

These protozoal infections usually affect puppies, especially in places where large numbers of puppies are brought together. Older dogs may harbor these infections but do

Whipworms are hard to find, and it is a job best left to a veterinarian. Pictured here are adult whipworms.

not show signs unless they are stressed. Symptoms include diarrhea, weight loss and lack of appetite. These infections are not always apparent in the fecal examination.

Tapeworms

Seldom apparent on fecal floatation, they are diagnosed frequently as rice-like segments around the dog's anus and the base of the tail. Tapeworms are long, flat and ribbon like, sometimes several feet in length, and made up of many segments about five-eighths of an inch long. The two most common types of tapeworms found in the dog are:

(1) First the larval form of the flea tapeworm parasite must mature in an intermediate host, the flea, before it can become infective. Your dog acquires this by ingesting the flea through licking and chewing.

(2) Rabbits, rodents and certain large game animals serve as intermediate hosts for other species of tapeworms. If your dog should eat one of these infected hosts, then he can acquire tapeworms.

Heartworm Disease

This is a worm that resides in the heart and adjacent blood vessels of the lung that produces microfilaria, which circulate in the bloodstream. It is possible for a dog to be infected with any number of worms from one to a hundred that can be 6 to

14 inches long. It is a life-threatening disease, expensive to treat and easily prevented. Depending on where you live, your veterinarian may recommend a preventive year-round and either an annual or semiannual blood test. The most common preventive is given once a month.

EXTERNAL PARASITES

Fleas

These pests are not only the dog's worst enemy but also enemy to the owner's pocketbook. Preventing is less expensive than treating, but regardless we'd prefer to spend our money elsewhere. Likely, the majority of our dogs are allergic to the bite of a flea, and in many cases it only takes one flea bite. The protein in the flea's saliva is the culprit. Allergic dogs have a reaction, which usually results in a "hot spot." More than likely such a reaction will involve a trip to the veterinarian for treatment. Yes, prevention is less expensive. Fortunately today there are several good products available.

If there is a flea infestation, no one product is going to correct the problem. Not only will the dog require treatment so will the environment. In general flea collars are not very effective although there is now available an "egg" collar that will kill the eggs on the dog. Dips are the most economical but they are messy. There are some effective shampoos and treatments available through pet shops and veterinarians. An oral tablet arrived on the American market in 1995 and was popular in Europe the previous year. It sterilizes the female flea

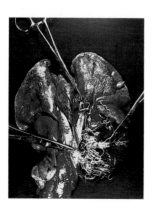

Dirofilaria— adult worms in the heart of a dog. Courtesy of Merck AgVet.

but will not kill adult fleas. Therefore the tablet, which is given monthly, will decrease the flea population but is not a "cure-all." Those dogs that suffer from flea-bite allergy will still be subjected to the bite of the flea. Another popular parasiticide is permethrin, which is applied to the back of the dog in one or two places depending on the dog's

The cat flea is the most common flea of both dogs and cats. Courtesy of Fleabusters, Rx for Fleas, Inc., Fort Lauderdale, Florida.

weight. This product works as a repellent causing the flea to get "hot feet" and jump off. Do not confuse this product with some of the organophosphates that are also applied to the dog's back.

Some products are not usable on young puppies. Treating fleas should be done under your veterinarian's guidance. Frequently it is necessary to combine products and the layman does not have the knowledge regarding possible toxicities. It is hard to believe but there are a few dogs that do have a natural resistance to fleas. Nevertheless it would be wise to treat all pets at the same time. Don't forget your cats. Cats just love to prowl the neighborhood and consequently return with unwanted guests.

Adult fleas live on the dog but their eggs drop off the dog into the environment. There they go through four larval stages before reaching adulthood, and thereby are able to jump back on the poor unsuspecting dog. The cycle resumes and takes between 21 to 28 days under ideal conditions. There are environmental products available that will kill both the adult fleas and the larvae.

Ticks

Ticks carry Rocky Mountain Spotted Fever, Lyme disease and can cause tick paralysis. They should be removed with tweezers, trying to pull out the head. The jaws carry disease. There is a tick preventive collar that does an excellent job. The ticks automatically back out on those dogs wearing collars.

Sarcoptic Mange

This is a mite that is difficult to find on skin scrapings. The pinnal reflex is a good indicator of this disease. Rub the ends of the pinna (ear) together and the dog will start scratching with his foot. Sarcoptes are highly contagious to other dogs and to humans although they do not live long on humans. They cause intense itching.

Demodectic Mange

This is a mite that is passed from the dam to her puppies. It affects youngsters age three to ten months. Diagnosis is confirmed by skin scraping. Small areas of alopecia around the eyes, lips and/or forelegs become visible. There is little itching unless there is a secondary bacterial infection. Some breeds are afflicted more than others.

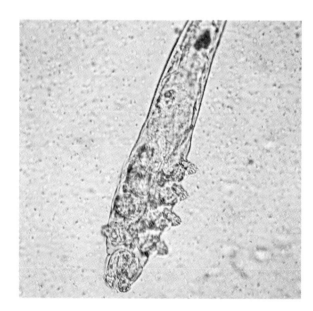

Demodectic mange is passed from a dam to her puppies. It involves areas of hair loss.

Cheyletiella

This causes intense itching and is diagnosed by skin scraping. It lives in the outer layers of the skin of dogs, cats, rabbits and humans. Yellow-gray scales may be found on the back and the rump, top of the head and the nose.

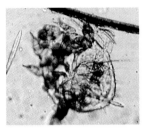

Sarcoptic mange is highly contagious to other dogs as well as humans. Sarcoptes cause intense itching.

To Breed or Not To Breed

More than likely your breeder has requested that you have your puppy neutered or spayed. Your breeder's request is based on what is healthiest for your dog and what is most beneficial for your breed. Experienced and conscientious breeders devote many years into

All Bull Terrier puppies are cute, but not all are of breeding quality. Reputable breeders will often sell pet-quality pups on the condition that they are spayed or neutered.

developing a bloodline. In order to do this, he makes every effort to plan each breeding in regard to conformation, temperament and health. This type of breeder does his best to perform the necessary testing (i.e., OFA, CERF, testing for inherited blood disorders, thyroid, etc.). Testing is expensive and sometimes very disheartening when a favorite dog doesn't pass his health tests. The health history pertains not only to the breeding stock but to the immediate ancestors. Reputable breeders do not want their offspring to be bred indiscriminately. Therefore you may be asked to neuter or spay your puppy. Of course there is always the exception, and your breeder may agree to let you breed your dog under his direct supervision. This is an important concept. More and more effort is being made to breed healthier dogs.

Spay/Neuter

There are numerous benefits of performing this surgery at six months of age. Unspayed females are subject to mammary and ovarian cancer. In order to prevent mammary cancer she must be spayed prior to her first heat cycle. Later in life, an unspayed

Breeding dogs of only the best quality assures that good health and temperament are passed down to each new generation.

Spaying/neutering is often the best option for your family pet. The health benefits are numerous and it will minimize the risk of certain diseases.

female may develop a pyometra (an infected uterus), which is definitely life threatening.

Spaying is performed under a general anesthetic and is easy on the young dog. As you might expect it is a little harder on the older dog, but that is no reason to deny her the surgery. The surgery removes the ovaries and uterus. It is important to remove all the ovarian tissue. If some is left behind, she could remain attractive to males. In order to view the ovaries, a reasonably long incision is necessary. An ovariohysterectomy is considered major surgery.

Neutering the male at a young age will inhibit some characteristic male behavior that owners frown upon. Some boys will not hike their legs and mark territory if they are neutered at six months of age. Also neutering at a young age has hormonal benefits, lessening the chance of hormonal aggressiveness.

Surgery involves removing the testicles but leaving the scrotum. If there should be a retained testicle, then he definitely needs to be neutered before the age of two or three years. Retained testicles can develop into cancer. Unneutered males are at risk for testicular cancer, perineal fistulas, perianal tumors and fistulas and prostatic disease.

Intact males and females are prone to housebreaking accidents. Females urinate frequently before, during and after heat cycles, and males tend to mark territory if there is a female in heat. Males may show the same behavior if there is a visiting dog or guests.

Surgery involves a sterile operating procedure equivalent to human surgery. The incision site is shaved, surgically scrubbed and draped. The veterinarian wears a sterile surgical gown, cap, mask and gloves. Anesthesia should be monitored by a registered technician. It is customary for the veterinarian to recommend a pre-anesthetic blood screening, looking for metabolic problems and a ECG rhythm strip to check for normal heart function. Today anesthetics are equal to human anesthetics, which enable your dog to walk out of the clinic the same day as surgery.

The Galileo™ is the toughest nylon bone ever made. It is flavored to appeal to your Bull Terrier and has a relatively soft outer layer. It is a necessary chew toy and doggy pacifier.

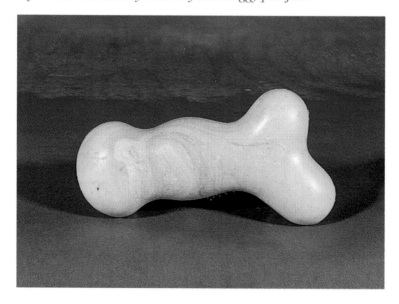

Some folks worry about their dog gaining weight after being neutered or spayed. This is usually not the case. It is true that some dogs may be less active so they could develop a problem, but most dogs are just as active as they were before surgery. However, if your dog should begin to gain, then you need to decrease his food and see to it that he gets a little more exercise.

Young pups are especially vulnerable to contagious diseases. Make sure your Bull Terrier pup has been vaccinated before taking him out to make friends.

Author Betty Desmond with "BabyFace" and "Red Rocket" show the benefits of pet ownership—love and companionship.

DENTAL CARE for Your Dog's Life

So you've got a new puppy! You also have a new set of puppy teeth in your household. Anyone who has ever raised a puppy is abundantly aware of these new teeth. Your puppy will chew anything it can reach, chase your shoelaces, and play "tear the rag" with any piece of clothing it can find. When puppies are newly born, they have no teeth. At about four weeks of age, puppies of most breeds begin to develop their deciduous or baby teeth. They begin eating semi-solid food, fighting and biting with their litter mates, and learning discipline from their mother. As their new teeth come in, they inflict more pain on their mother's breasts, so her feeding sessions become less frequent and shorter. By six or eight weeks, the mother will start growling to warn her pups when they are fighting too roughly or hurting her as they nurse too much with their new teeth.

Puppies need to chew. It is a necessary part of their physical and mental development. They develop muscles and necessary life skills as they drag objects around, fight over possession, and vocalize alerts and warnings. Puppies chew on things to explore their world. They are using their sense of taste to determine what is food and what is not. How else can they tell an electrical cord from a lizard? At about four months of age, most puppies begin shedding their baby teeth. Often these

Raised dental tips on the surface of every Plaque Attacker® bone help to combat plaque and tartar. Safe for aggressive chewers and ruggedly constructed to last, Plaque Attacker® dental bones provide hours and hours of tooth-saving enjoyment.

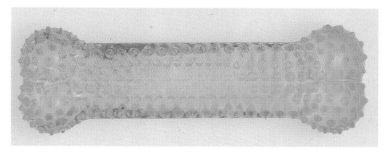

teeth need some help to come out and make way for the permanent teeth. The incisors (front teeth) will be replaced first. Then, the adult canine or fang teeth erupt. When the baby tooth is not shed before the permanent tooth comes in, veterinarians call it a retained deciduous tooth. This condition will often cause gum infections by trapping hair and debris between the permanent tooth and the retained baby tooth. Nylafloss® is an excellent device for puppies to use. They can toss it, drag it, and chew on the many surfaces it presents. The baby teeth can catch in the nylon material, aiding in their removal. Puppies that have adequate chew toys will have less destructive behavior, develop more physically, and have less chance of retained deciduous teeth.

Brushing your dog's teeth is recommended by every veterinarian. Use the 2-Brush® regularly, 3-4 times per week and you may never need your veterinarian to do the job for you.

During the first year, your dog should be seen by your veterinarian at regular intervals. Your veterinarian will let you know when to bring in your puppy for vaccinations and parasite examinations. At each visit, your veterinarian should inspect the lips, teeth, and mouth as part of a complete physical examination. You should take some part in the maintenance of your dog's oral health. You should examine your dog's mouth weekly throughout his first year to make sure there are no sores, foreign objects, tooth problems, etc. If your dog drools excessively, shakes its head, or has bad breath, consult your veterinarian. By the time your dog is six months old, the permanent teeth are all in and plaque can start to accumulate on the tooth surfaces. This is when your dog needs to develop good dental-care habits to prevent calculus build-up on its teeth. Brushing is best. That is a fact that cannot be denied. However, some dogs do not like their teeth brushed regularly, or you may not be able to accomplish the task. In that case, you should consider a product that will help prevent plaque and calculus build-up.

The Plaque Attackers® and Galileo Bone® are other excellent choices for the first three years of a dog's life. Their shapes make them interesting for the dog. As the dog chews on them, the solid polyurethane massages the gums which improves the blood circulation to the periodontal tissues. Projections on the chew devices increase the surface and are in contact with the tooth for more efficient cleaning. The unique shape and consistency prevent your dog from exerting excessive force on his own teeth or from breaking off pieces of the bone. If your dog is an aggressive chewer or weighs more than 55 pounds (25 kg), you should consider giving him a Nylabone®, the most durable chew product on the market.

The Gumabones ®, made by the Nylabone Company, are constructed of strong polyurethane, which is softer than nylon. Less powerful chewers prefer the Gumabones® to the Nylabones®. A super option for your dog is the Hercules Bone®, a uniquely shaped bone named after the great Olympian for its exceptional strength. Like all Nylabone products, they are specially scented to make them attractive to your dog. Ask your veterinarian about these bones and he will validate the good doctor's prescription: Nylabones® not only give your dog a good chewing workout but also help to save your dog's teeth (and even his life, as it protects him from possible fatal periodontal diseases).

By the time dogs are four years old, 75% of them have periodontal disease. It is the

There is only one material suitable for flossing human teeth and that's nylon. So why not get a chew toy that will enable you to interact with your Bull Terrier while it promotes dental health. As you play tug-of-war with a Nylafloss®, you'll be slowly pulling the nylon strand through your dog's teeth.

most common infection in dogs. Yearly examinations by your veterinarian are essential to maintaining your dog's good health. If your veterinarian detects periodontal disease, he or she may recommend a prophylactic cleaning. To do a thorough cleaning, it will be necessary to put your dog under anesthesia. With modern gas anesthetics and monitoring equipment, the procedure is pretty safe. Your veterinarian will scale the teeth with an ultrasound scaler or hand instrument. This removes the calculus from the teeth. If there are calculus deposits below the gum line, the veterinarian

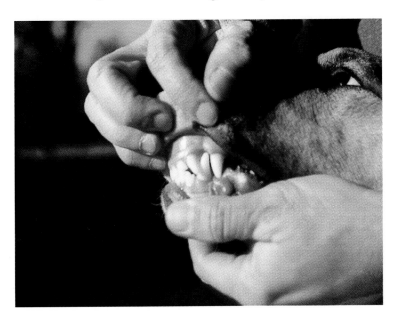

If you accustom your puppy to oral examination at an early age, tasks like brushing his teeth will be much easier in the future.

A thorough examination of your Bull Terrier's mouth, teeth, and gums should be part of his annual checkup.

will plane the roots to make them smooth. After all of the calculus has been removed, the teeth are polished with pumice in a polishing cup. If any medical or surgical treatment is needed, it is done at this time. The final step would be fluoride treatment and your follow-up treatment at home. If the periodontal disease is advanced, the veterinarian may prescribe a medicated mouth rinse or antibiotics for use at home. Make sure your dog has safe, clean and attractive chew toys and treats. Chooz® treats are another way of using a consumable treat to help keep your dog's teeth clean.

Rawhide is the most popular of all materials for a dog to chew. This has never been good news to dog owners, because rawhide is inherently very dangerous for dogs. Thousands of dogs have died from rawhide, having swallowed the hide after it has become soft and mushy, only to cause stomach and intestinal blockage. A new rawhide product on the market has finally solved the problem of rawhide: molded Roar-Hide® from Nylabone. These are composed of processed, cut up, and melted American rawhide injected into your dog's favorite shape: a dog bone. These

If your Bull Terrier would rather chew than do anything else, the Gumabone® is for him. Offer him a Gumabone® made of non-toxic, durable polyurethane to sink his teeth into.

dog-safe devices smell and taste like rawhide but don't break up. The ridges on the bones help to fight tartar build-up on the teeth and they last ten times longer than the usual rawhide chews.

As your dog ages, professional examination and cleaning should become more frequent. The mouth should be inspected at least once a year. Your veterinarian may recommend visits every six months. In the geriatric patient, organs such as the heart, liver, and kidneys do not function as well as when they were young. Your veterinarian will probably want to test these organs' functions prior to using general anesthesia for dental cleaning. If your dog is a good chewer and you work closely with your veterinarian, your dog can keep all of its teeth all of its life. However, as your dog ages, his sense of smell, sight, and taste will diminish. He may not have the desire to chase, trap or chew his toys. He will also not have the energy to chew for long periods, as arthritis and periodontal disease make chewing painful. This will leave you with more responsibility for keeping his teeth clean and healthy. The dog that would not let you brush his teeth at one year of age, may let you brush his teeth now that he is ten years old.

If you train your dog with good chewing habits as a puppy, he will have healthier teeth throughout his life.

Your puppy deserves the best! Provide him with plenty of safe and healthy chew toys while he is teething, like this Nylabone® Frisbee™.

117

TRAVELING with Your Dog

The earlier you start traveling with your new puppy or dog, the better. He needs to become accustomed to traveling. However, some dogs are nervous riders and become carsick easily. It is helpful if he starts with an empty stomach. Do not despair, as it will go better if you continue taking him with you on short fun rides. How would you feel if every time you rode in the car you stopped at the doctor's for an injection? You would soon dread that nasty car. Older dogs that tend to get carsick may have more of a problem adjusting to traveling. Those dogs that are having a serious problem may benefit from some medication prescribed by the veterinarian.

Before any car excursion be sure your puppy is allowed plenty of time outdoors to attend to his needs.

Do give your dog a chance to relieve himself before getting into the car. It is a good idea to be prepared for a clean up with a leash, paper towels, bag and terry cloth towel.

The safest place for your dog is in a fiberglass crate, although close confinement can promote carsickness in some dogs. If your dog is nervous you can try letting him ride on the seat next to you or in someone's lap.

An alternative to the crate would be to use a car harness made for dogs and/or a safety strap attached to the harness or collar. Whatever you do, do not let your dog ride in the back of a pickup truck unless he is securely tied on a very short lead. I've seen trucks stop quickly and, even though the dog was

The earlier you take your Bull Terriers traveling with you, the quicker they will become accustomed to riding in a car.

tied, it fell out and was dragged.

Another advantage of the crate is that it is a safe place to leave him if you need to run into the store. Otherwise you wouldn't be able to leave the windows down. Keep in mind that while many dogs are overly protective in their crates, this may not be enough to deter dognappers. In some states it is against the law to leave a dog in the car unattended.

Never leave a dog loose in the car wearing a collar and leash. More than one dog has killed himself by hanging. Do not let him put his head out an open window. Foreign debris can be blown into his eyes. When leaving your dog unattended in a car, consider the temperature. It can take less than five minutes to reach temperatures over 100 degrees Fahrenheit.

Trips

Perhaps you are taking a trip. Give consideration to what is best for your dog–traveling with you or boarding. When traveling by car, van or motor home, you need to think ahead about locking your vehicle. In all probability you have many valuables in the car and do not wish to leave it unlocked. Perhaps most valuable and not replaceable is your dog. Give thought to securing your vehicle and providing adequate ventilation for him. Another consideration for you when traveling with your dog is medical problems that may arise and little inconveniences, such as exposure to external parasites. Some areas of the country are quite flea infested. You may want to carry flea spray with you. This is even a good idea when staying in motels. Quite possibly you are not the only occupant of the room.

Unbelievably many motels and even hotels do allow canine guests, even some very first-class ones. Gaines Pet Foods Corporation publishes *Touring With Towser*, a directory of domestic hotels and motels that accommodate guests with dogs. Their address is

Crates are a safe way for your dog to travel. The fiberglass crates are the safest for air travel, but the metal crates allow for better air circulation.

Gaines TWT, PO Box 5700, Kankakee, IL, 60902. Call ahead to any motel that you may be considering and see if they accept pets. Sometimes it is necessary to pay a deposit against room damage. The management may feel reassured if you mention that

A reputable boarding kennel will require that dogs receive the vaccination for kennel cough no less than two weeks before their scheduled stay.

your dog will be crated. If you do travel with your dog, take along plenty of baggies so that you can clean up after him. When we all do our share in cleaning up, we make it possible for motels to continue accepting our pets. As a matter of fact, you should practice cleaning up everywhere you take your dog.

Depending on where your are traveling, you may need an up-to-date health certificate issued by your veterinarian. It is good policy to take along your dog's medical information, which would include the name, address and phone number of your veterinarian, vaccination record, rabies certificate, and any medication he is taking.

Air Travel

When traveling by air, you need to contact the airlines to check their policy. Usually you have to make arrangements up to a couple of weeks in advance for traveling with your dog. The airlines require your dog to travel in an airline approved fiberglass crate. Usually these can be purchased through the airlines but they are also readily available in most pet-supply stores. If your dog is not accustomed to a crate, then it is a good idea to get him acclimated to it before your trip. The day of the actual trip you should withhold water about one hour ahead of departure and no food for about 12 hours. The airlines generally have temperature restrictions, which do not allow pets to travel if it is either too cold or too hot. Frequently these restrictions are based on the temperatures at the departure and arrival airports. It's best to inquire about a health certificate. These usually need to be issued within ten days of departure. You should arrange for non-stop, direct flights and if a commuter plane should be involved, check to see if it will carry dogs. Some don't. The Humane Society of the United States has put together a tip sheet for airline traveling. You can receive a copy by sending a self-addressed stamped envelope to:

Make sure your Bull Terrier wears a collar with tags at all times. This will increase your chances of being reunited should you become separated.

The Humane Society of the United States
Tip Sheet
2100 L Street NW
Washington, DC 20037.

Regulations differ for traveling outside of the country and are sometimes changed without notice. Well in advance you need to write or call the appropriate consulate or agricultural department for instructions. Some countries have lengthy quarantines (six months), and countries differ in their rabies vaccination requirements. For instance, it may have to be given at least 30 days ahead of your departure.

Do make sure your dog is wearing proper identification including your name, phone number and city. You never know when you might be in an accident and separated from your dog. Or your dog could be frightened and somehow manage to escape and run away.

If you decide to bring your Bull Terriers with you when you travel, bring along some familiar things, like a bed and toys, to make them feel more at home.

Another suggestion would be to carry in-case-of-emergency instructions. These would include the address and phone number of a relative or friend, your veterinarian's name, address and phone number, and your dog's medical information.

BOARDING KENNELS

Perhaps you have decided that you need to board your dog. Your veterinarian can recommend a good boarding facility or possibly a pet sitter that will come to your house. It is customary for the boarding kennel to ask for proof of vaccination for the DHLPP, rabies and bordetella vaccine. The bordetella should have been given within six months of boarding. This is for your protection. If they do not ask for this proof I would not board at their kennel. Ask about flea control. Those dogs that suffer flea-bite allergy can get in trouble at a boarding kennel. Unfortunately boarding kennels are limited on how much they are able to do.

For more information on pet sitting, contact NAPPS:
National Association of
Professional Pet Sitters
   1200 G Street, NW
   Suite 760
   Washington, DC 20005.

The well-adjusted Bull Terrier can make himself comfortable anywhere!

Some pet clinics have technicians that pet sit and technicians that board clinic patients in their homes. This may be an alternative for you. Ask your veterinarian if they have an employee that can help you. There is a definite advantage of having a technician care for your dog, especially if your dog is on medication or is a senior citizen.

You can write for a copy of *Traveling With Your Pet* from ASPCA, Education Department,

If your Bull Terrier is more comfortable at home when you travel, there are many reputable pet-sitting services available in your area.

Your puppy's safety and well being is important to you, so be sure to inquire about airline and hotel regulations before making travel plans.

441 E. 92nd Street, New York, NY 10128.

IDENTIFICATION and Finding the Lost Dog

There are several ways of identifying your dog. The old standby is a collar with dog license, rabies, and ID tags. Unfortunately collars have a way of being separated from the dog and tags fall off. We're not suggesting you shouldn't use a collar and tags. If they stay intact and on the dog, they are the quickest way of identification.

For several years owners have been tattooing their dogs. Some tattoos use a number with a registry. Here lies the problem because there are several registries to check. If you wish to tattoo, use your social security number. The humane shelters have the means to trace it. It is usually done on the inside of the rear thigh. The area is first shaved and numbed. There is no pain, although a few dogs do not like the buzzing sound. Occasionally tattooing is not legible and needs to be redone.

The newest method of identification is microchipping. The microchip is no bigger than a grain of rice.

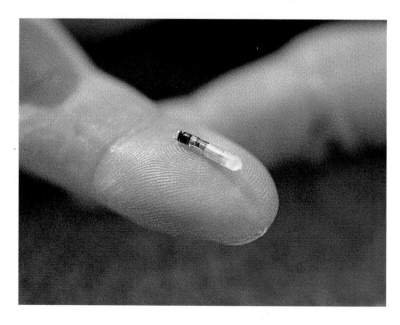

126

The newest method of identification is microchipping. The microchip is a computer chip that is no larger than a grain of rice. The veterinarian implants it by injection between the shoulder blades. The dog feels no discomfort. If your dog is lost and picked up by the humane society, they can trace you by scanning the microchip, which has its own code. Microchip scanners are friendly to other brands of microchips and their registries. The microchip comes with a dog tag saying the dog is microchipped. It is the safest way of identifying your dog.

FINDING THE LOST DOG

I am sure you will agree that there would be little worse than losing your dog. Responsible pet owners rarely lose their dogs. They do not let their dogs run free because they don't want harm to come to them. Not only that but in most, if not all, states there is a leash law.

Beware of fenced-in yards. They can be a hazard. Dogs find ways to escape either over or under the fence. Another fast exit is through the gate that perhaps the neighbor's child left unlocked.

Below is a list that hopefully will be of help to you if you need it. Remember don't give up, keep looking. Your dog is worth your efforts.

1. Contact your neighbors and put flyers with a photo on it in their mailboxes. Information you should include would be the dog's name, breed, sex, color, age, source of identification, when your dog was last seen and where, and your name and phone

Be sure to provide your Bull Terrier with a large fenced-in yard so he has a safe area to roam.

Your Bull Terrier will be curious about his environment and other dogs when you take him out. Always keep him on a lead to prevent him from wandering off without you.

numbers. It may be helpful to say the dog needs medical care. Offer a *reward*.

2. Check all local shelters daily. It is also possible for your dog to be picked up away from home and end up in an out-of-the-way shelter. Check these too. Go in person. It is not good enough to call. Most shelters are limited on the time they can hold dogs then they are put up for adoption or euthanized. There is the possibility that your dog will not make it to the shelter for several days. Your dog could have been wandering or someone may have tried to keep him.

3. Notify all local veterinarians. Call and send flyers.

4. Call your breeder. Frequently breeders are contacted when one of their breed is found.

5. Contact the rescue group for your breed.

6. Contact local schools—children may have seen your dog.

7. Post flyers at the schools, groceries, gas stations, convenience stores, veterinary clinics, groomers and any other place that will allow them.

8. Advertise in the newspaper.

9. Advertise on the radio.

BEHAVIOR and Canine Communication

Studies of the human/animal bond point out the importance of the unique relationships that exist between people and their pets. Those of us who share our lives with pets understand the special part they play through companionship, service and protection. For many, the pet/owner bond goes beyond simple companionship; pets are often considered members of the family. A leading pet food manufacturer recently conducted a nationwide survey of pet owners to gauge just how important pets were in their lives. Here's what they found:

- 76 percent allow their pets to sleep on their beds
- 78 percent think of their pets as their children
- 84 percent display photos of their pets, mostly in their homes
- 84 percent think that their pets react to their own emotions
- 100 percent talk to their pets
- 97 percent think that their pets understand what they're saying

Many people thrive on the devoted companionship a Bull Terrier can provide. Jim Arrington and Ch. Ann Dee's Crimson Tide agree.

Are you surprised?

Senior citizens show more concern for their own eating habits when they have the responsibility of feeding a dog. Seeing that their dog is routinely exercised encourages the owner to think of schedules that otherwise may seem unimportant to the senior citizen. The older owner may be arthritic and feeling poorly but with responsibility for his dog he has a reason to get up

Puppies will find mischief whenever possible! You will have to play the role of pack leader in order to teach your Bull Terrier appropriate behavior.

and get moving. It is a big plus if his dog is an attention seeker who will demand such from his owner.

Over the last couple of decades, it has been shown that pets relieve the stress of those who lead busy lives. Owning a pet has been known to lessen the occurrence of heart attack and stroke.

Many single folks thrive on the companionship of a dog. Lifestyles are very different from a long time ago, and today more individuals seek the single life. However, they receive fulfillment from owning a dog.

Most likely the majority of our dogs live in family environments. The companionship they provide is well worth the effort involved. In my opinion, every child should have the opportunity to have a family dog. Dogs teach responsibility through understanding their care, feelings and even respecting their life cycles. Frequently those children who have not been exposed to dogs grow up afraid of dogs, which isn't good. Dogs sense timidity and some will take advantage of the situation.

Today more dogs are serving as service dogs. Since the origination of the Seeing Eye dogs years ago, we now have trained hearing dogs. Also dogs are trained to provide service for the handicapped and are able to perform many different tasks for their owners. Search and Rescue dogs, with their handlers, are sent throughout the world to assist in recovery of disaster victims. They are life savers.

With the proper supervision, your puppy should be allowed to experience and explore his surroundings.

Therapy dogs are very popular with nursing homes, and some hospitals even allow them to visit. The inhabitants truly look forward to their visits. They wanted and were allowed to have visiting dogs in their beds to hold and love.

Nationally there is a Pet Awareness Week to educate students and others about the value and basic care of our pets. Many countries take an even greater interest in their pets than Americans do. In those countries the pets are allowed to accompany their owners into restaurants

People who are exposed to dogs learn to love, understand, and respect animals.

Although some traits are inherited within a breed, every Bull Terrier is an individual with his own personality—this little reindeer agrees!

and shops, etc. In the U.S. this freedom is only available to our service dogs. Even so we think very highly of the human/animal bond.

133

CANINE BEHAVIOR

Canine behavior problems are the number-one reason for pet owners to dispose of their dogs, either through new homes, humane shelters or euthanasia. Unfortunately there are too many owners who are unwilling to devote the necessary time to properly train their dogs. On the other hand, there are those who not only are concerned about inherited health problems but are also aware of the dog's mental stability.

You may realize that a breed and his group relatives (i.e., sporting, hounds, etc.) show tendencies to behavioral characteristics. An experienced breeder can acquaint you with his breed's personality. Unfortunately many breeds are labeled with poor temperaments when actually the breed as a whole is not affected but only a small percentage of individuals within the breed.

Inheritance and environment contribute to the dog's behavior. Some naïve people suggest inbreeding as the cause of bad

Most Bull Terriers become family members and must learn to conform to the rules of the household.

Puppies need proper training and socialization from the very beginning to become a welcome and valued member of your household.

temperaments. Inbreeding only results in poor behavior if the ancestors carry the trait. If there are excellent temperaments behind the dogs, then inbreeding will promote good temperaments in the offspring. Did you ever consider that inbreeding is what sets the characteristics of a breed? A purebred dog is the end result of inbreeding. This does not spare the mixed-breed dog from the same problems. Mixed-breed dogs frequently are the offspring of purebred dogs.

Not too many decades ago most of our dogs led a different lifestyle than what is prevalent today. Usually mom stayed home so the dog had human companionship and someone to discipline it if needed. Not much was expected from the dog. Today's mom works and everyone's life is at a much faster pace.

The dog may have to adjust to being a "weekend" dog. The family is gone all day during the week, and the dog is left to his own devices for entertainment. Some dogs sleep all day waiting for their family to come home and others become wigwam wreckers if given the opportunity. Crates do ensure the safety of the dog and the house. However, he could become a physical and emotional cripple if he doesn't get enough exercise and attention. We still appreciate and want the companionship of our dogs although we expect more from them. In many cases we tend to forget dogs are just that—*dogs* not human beings.

SOCIALIZING AND TRAINING

Many prospective puppy buyers lack experience regarding the proper socialization and training needed to develop the type of pet we all desire. In the first 18 months, training does take some work. It is easier to start proper training before there is a problem that needs to be corrected.

The initial work begins with the breeder. The breeder should start socializing the puppy at five to six weeks of age and cannot let up. Human socializing is critical up through 12 weeks of age and likewise important during the following months. The litter should be left together during the first few weeks but it is necessary to separate them by ten weeks of age. Leaving them together after that time will increase competition

Your puppy's relationship with his littermates is an essential one. He will learn to interact with other dogs by playing with his siblings.

136

for litter dominance. If puppies are not socialized with people by 12 weeks of age, they will be timid in later life.

The eight- to ten-week age period is a fearful time for puppies. They need to be handled very gently around children and adults. There should be no harsh discipline during this time. Starting at 14 weeks of age, the puppy begins the

Puppies should be socialized with their littermates until they are about 10 weeks old, then separated and introduced to outsiders.

Behavior and health problems can be passed down from generation to generation, so be sure to check your puppy's lineage very carefully.

juvenile period, which ends when he reaches sexual maturity around six to 14 months of age. During the juvenile period he needs to be introduced to strangers (adults, children and other dogs) on the home property. At sexual maturity he will begin to bark at strangers and become more protective. Males start to lift their legs to urinate but if you desire you can

Although Bull Terriers are not generally considered good cooks, they can lead lives of service—as trained aide dogs or as man's best friend!

inhibit this behavior by walking your boy on leash away from trees, shrubs, fences, etc.

Perhaps you are thinking about an older puppy. You need to inquire about the puppy's social experience. If he has lived in a kennel, he may have a hard time adjusting to people and environmental stimuli. Assuming he has had a good social upbringing, there are advantages to an older puppy.

Training includes puppy kindergarten and a minimum of one to two basic training classes. During these classes you will learn how to dominate your youngster. This is especially important if you own a large breed of dog. It is somewhat harder, if not nearly impossible, for some owners to be the Alpha figure when their dog towers over them. You will be taught how to properly restrain your dog. This concept is important. Again it puts you in the Alpha position. All dogs need to be restrained many times during their lives. Believe it or not, some of our worst offenders are the eight-week-old puppies that are brought to our clinic. They need to be gently restrained for a nail trim but the way they carry on you would think we were killing them. In comparison, their vaccination is a "piece of cake." When we ask dogs to do something that is not agreeable to them, then their worst comes out. Life will be easier for your dog if you expose him at a young age to the necessities of life—proper behavior and restraint.

Well-socialized puppies should be able to interact with each other without showing fear or aggression.

UNDERSTANDING THE DOG'S LANGUAGE

Most authorities agree that the dog is a descendent of the wolf. The dog and wolf have similar traits. For instance both are pack oriented and prefer not to be isolated for long periods of time. Another characteristic is that the dog, like the wolf, looks to the leader—Alpha—for direction. Both the wolf and the dog communicate through body language, not only within their pack but with outsiders.

Every pack has an Alpha figure. The dog looks to you, or should look to you, to be that leader. If your dog doesn't receive the proper training and guidance, he very well may replace you as Alpha. This would be a serious problem and is certainly a disservice to your dog.

Eye contact is one way the Alpha wolf keeps order within his pack. You are Alpha so you must establish eye contact with your puppy. Obviously your puppy will have to look at you. Practice eye contact even if you need to hold his head for five to ten seconds at a time. You can give him a treat as a reward. Make sure your eye contact is gentle and not threatening. Later, if he has been naughty, it is permissible to give him a

139

long, penetrating look. There are some older dogs that never learned eye contact as puppies and cannot accept eye contact. You should avoid eye contact with these dogs since they feel threatened and will retaliate as such.

BODY LANGUAGE

The play bow, when the forequarters are down and the hindquarters are elevated, is an invitation to play. Puppies play fight, which helps them learn the acceptable limits of biting. This is necessary for later in their lives. Nevertheless, an owner may be falsely reassured by the playful nature of his dog's aggression. Playful aggression toward another dog or human may be an indication of serious aggression in the future. Owners should never play fight or play tug-of-war with any dog that is inclined to be dominant.

Signs of submission are:
1. Avoids eye contact.
2. Active submission—the dog crouches down, ears back and the tail is lowered.
3. Passive submission—the dog rolls on his side with his hindlegs in the air and frequently urinates.
Signs of dominance are:
1. Makes eye contact.
2. Stands with ears up, tail up and the hair raised on his neck.

A lot can be learned about a Bull Terrier's behavior and attitude simply by observing his body language. This smiling guy looks happy to meet anyone.

A stable even-tempered Bull Terrier is one that is neither fearful nor aggressive.

3. Shows dominance over another dog by standing at right angles over it.

Dominant dogs tend to behave in characteristic ways such as:

1. The dog may be unwilling to move from his place (i.e., reluctant to give up the sofa if the owner wants to sit there).

2. He may not part with toys or objects in his mouth and may show possessiveness with his food bowl.

3. He may not respond quickly to commands.

4. He may be disagreeable for grooming and dislikes to be petted.

Dogs are popular because of their sociable nature. Those that have contact with humans during the first 12 weeks of life regard them as a member of their own species–their pack. All dogs have the potential for both dominant and submissive behavior. Only through experience and training do they learn to whom it is appropriate to show which behavior. Not all dogs are concerned with dominance but owners need to be aware of that potential. It is wise for the owner to establish his dominance early on.

A human can express dominance or submission toward a dog in the following ways:

It is important to remember that your Bull Terrier wants to please you and with patience, will learn what you have to teach him!

1. Meeting the dog's gaze signals dominance. Averting the gaze signals submission. If the dog growls or threatens, averting the gaze is the first avoiding action to take—it may prevent attack. It is important to establish eye contact in the puppy. The older dog that has not been exposed to eye contact may see it as a threat and will not be willing to submit.

2. Being taller than the dog signals dominance; being lower signals submission. This is why, when attempting to make friends with a strange dog or catch the runaway, one should kneel down to his level. Some owners see their dogs become dominant when allowed on the furniture or on the bed. Then he is at the owner's level.

3. An owner can gain dominance by ignoring all the dog's social initiatives. The owner pays attention to the dog only when he obeys a command.

No dog should be allowed to achieve dominant status over any adult or child. Ways of preventing are as follows:

1. Handle the puppy gently, especially during the three- to four-month period.

Dogs are popular because of their sociable nature, but a dog that displays dominance over his family will be difficult to train and hard to control.

2. Let the children and adults handfeed him and teach him to take food without lunging or grabbing.

3. Do not allow him to chase children or joggers.

4. Do not allow him to jump on people or mount their legs. Even females may be inclined to mount. It is not only a male habit.

5. Do not allow him to growl for any reason.

6. Don't participate in wrestling or tug-of-war games.

7. Don't physically punish puppies for aggressive behavior. Restrain him from repeating the infraction and teach an alternative behavior. Dogs should earn everything they receive from their owners. This would include sitting to receive petting or treats, sitting before going out the door and sitting to receive the collar and leash. These types of exercises reinforce the owner's dominance.

If your dog seems fearful of people or things, respect his feelings and give him time alone to get used to the situation.

Young children should never be left alone with a dog. It is important that children learn some basic obedience commands so they have some control over the dog. They will gain the respect of their dog.

FEAR

One of the most common problems dogs experience is being fearful. Some dogs are more afraid than others. On the lesser side, which is sometimes humorous to watch, dogs can be afraid of a strange object. They act silly when something is out of place in the house. We call his problem perceptive intelligence. He realizes the abnormal within his known environment. He does not react the same way in strange environments since he does not know what is normal.

On the more serious side is a fear of people. This can result in backing off, seeking his own space and saying "leave me

A puppy is a particularly social creature, and needs the company of other puppies when young. The more people and animals he meets, the better socialized he will become.

alone" or it can result in an aggressive behavior that may lead to challenging the person. Respect that the dog wants to be left alone and give him time to come forward. If you approach the cornered dog, he may resort to snapping. If you leave him alone, he may decide to come forward, which should be rewarded with a treat.

Some dogs may initially be too fearful to take treats. In these cases it is helpful to make sure the dog hasn't eaten for about 24 hours. Being a little hungry encourages him to accept the treats, especially if they are of the "gourmet" variety.

Dogs can be afraid of numerous things, including loud noises and thunderstorms. Invariably the owner rewards (by comforting) the dog when it shows signs of fearfulness. When your dog is frightened, direct his attention to something else and act happy. Don't dwell on his fright.

Aggression

Some different types of aggression are: predatory, defensive, dominant, possessive, protective, fear induced, noise provoked, "rage" syndrome (unprovoked aggression), maternal and aggression directed toward other dogs. Aggression is the most common behavioral problem encountered. Protective breeds are expected to be more aggressive than others but with the proper upbringing they can make very dependable companions. You need to be able to read your dog.

Many factors contribute to aggression including genetics and environment. An improper environment, which may include the living conditions, lack of social life, excessive punishment, being attacked or frightened by an aggressive dog, etc., can all influence a dog's behavior. Even spoiling him and giving too much praise may be detrimental. Isolation and the lack of human contact or exposure to frequent teasing by children or adults also can ruin a good dog.

Lack of direction, fear, or confusion lead to aggression in those dogs that are so inclined. Any obedience exercise, even the sit and down, can direct the dog and overcome fear and/or confusion. Every dog should learn these commands as a youngster, and there should be periodic reinforcement.

When a dog is showing signs of aggression, you should speak calmly (no screaming or hysterics) and firmly give a command that he understands, such as the sit. As soon as your dog obeys, you have assumed your dominant position. Aggression presents a problem because there may be danger to others. Sometimes it is an emotional issue. Owners may consciously or unconsciously encourage their dog's aggression. Other owners show responsibility by accepting the problem and taking measures to keep it under control. The owner is

An unwillingness to give up his toys may signal that your dog is displaying dominant tendencies. Your Bull Terrier must always know that you are the boss.

responsible for his dog's actions, and it is not wise to take a chance on someone being bitten, especially a child. Euthanasia is the solution for some owners and in severe cases this may be the best choice. However, few dogs are that dangerous and very few are that much of a threat to their owners.

Bull Terriers love to play tug-of-war, however if either dog becomes aggressive, put an end to the game immediately.

If caution is exercised and professional help is gained early on, most cases can be controlled.

Teach your Bull Terrier how you want him to behave. Practicing training and obedience exercises will further demonstrate your dominance.

Some authorities recommend feeding a lower protein (less than 20 percent) diet. They believe this can aid in reducing aggression. If the dog loses

weight, then vegetable oil can be added. Veterinarians and behaviorists are having some success with pharmacology. In many cases treatment is possible and can improve the situation.

If you have done everything according to "the book" regarding training and socializing and are still having a behavior problem, don't procrastinate. It is important that the problem gets attention before it is out of hand. It is estimated that 20 percent of a veterinarian's time may be devoted to dealing with problems before they become so intolerable that the dog is separated from its home and owner. If your veterinarian isn't able to help, he should refer you to a behaviorist.

Excessive barking can be an annoyance, but dogs also use their bark to "verbally" communicate. What is your Bull Terrier trying to tell you?

PROBLEMS

Barking

This is a habit that shouldn't be encouraged. Some owners desire their dog to bark so as to be a watchdog. Most dogs will bark when a stranger comes to the door.

The new puppy frequently barks or whines in the crate in his strange environment and the owner reinforces the puppy's bad behavior by going to him during the night. This is a no-no. Smack the top of the crate and say "quiet" in a loud, firm voice. The puppies don't like to hear the loud noise of the crate being banged. If the barking is sleep-interrupting, then the owner should take crate and pup to the bedroom for a few days until the puppy becomes adjusted to his new environment. Otherwise ignore the barking during the night.

Barking can be an inherited problem or a bad habit learned through the environment. It takes dedication to stop the barking. Attention should be paid to the cause of the barking. Does the dog seek attention, does he need to go

Dogs often jump up as a sign of affection. However, your Bull Terrier must learn that not everyone will appreciate paw prints on their clothes!

out, is it feeding time, is it occurring when he is left alone, is it a protective bark, etc.? Overzealous barking is an inherited tendency. When barking presents a problem for you, try to stop it as soon as it begins.

There are electronic collars available that are supposed to curb barking. There are some disadvantages to to the collar. If the dog is barking out of excitement, punishment is not the appropriate treatment. Presumably there is the chance the collar could be activated by other stimuli and thereby punish the dog when it is not barking. Should you decide to use one, then you should seek help from a person with experience with that type of collar. Nevertheless the root of the problem needs to be investigated and corrected.

In extreme circumstances (usually when there is a problem with the neighbors), some people have resorted to having their dogs debarked. I caution you that the dog continues to bark but usually only a squeaking sound is heard. Frequently the vocal cords

Bull Terriers love to be in on the action and will often jump up to get a better look. However, your Bully must learn that good manners are a necessary at all times!

Bull Terriers love snacks, but they must learn never to help themselves!

grow back. Probably the biggest concern is that the dog can be left with scar tissue which can narrow the opening to the trachea.

Jumping Up

A dog that jumps up is a happy dog. Nevertheless few guests appreciate dogs jumping on them. Clothes get footprinted and/or snagged.

Some trainers believe in allowing the puppy to jump up during his first few weeks. If you correct him too soon and at the wrong age you may intimidate him. Consequently he could be timid around humans later in his life. However, there will come a time, probably around four months of age, that he needs to know when it is okay to jump and when he is to show off good manners by sitting instead.

Some authorities never allow jumping. If you are irritated by your dog jumping up on you, then you should discourage it from the beginning. A larger breed of dog can cause harm to a senior citizen. Some are quite fragile. It may not take much to cause a topple that could break a hip.

How do you correct the problem? All family members need to participate in teaching the puppy to sit as soon as he starts to jump up. The sit must be practiced every time he starts to jump up. Don't forget to praise him for his good behavior. If an older dog has acquired the habit, grasp his paws and squeeze tightly. Give a firm "No." He'll soon catch on. Remember the entire family must take part. Each time you allow him to jump up you go back a step in training.

Biting

All puppies bite and try to chew on your fingers, toes, arms, etc. This is the time to teach them to be gentle and not bite hard. Put your fingers in your puppy's mouth and if he bites too hard then say "easy" and let him know he's hurting you. Squeal and act like you have been seriously hurt. If the puppy plays too rough and doesn't respond to your corrections, then he needs "Time Out" in his crate. You should be particularly careful with young children and puppies who still have their deciduous (baby) teeth. Those teeth are like needles and can leave little scars on youngsters.

Your Bull Terrier's relationship with other dogs is an essential one. These two puppies pose for a picture.

Keeping your puppies entertained and occupied with toys, like this Gumabone® Frisbee™, will help prevent them from getting into mischief.

Biting in the more mature dog is something that should be prevented at all costs. Should it occur quickly let him know in no uncertain terms that biting will not be tolerated. When biting is directed toward another dog (dog fight), don't get in the middle of it. Some authorities recommend breaking up a fight by elevating the hind legs. This would only be possible if there was a person for each dog. Obviously it would be hard to fight with the hind legs off the ground. A dog bite is serious and should be given attention. Wash the bite with soap and water and contact your doctor. It is important to know the status of the offender's rabies vaccination.

Your dog must know who is boss. When biting occurs, you should seek professional help at once. On the other hand you must not let your dog intimidate you and be so afraid of a bite that you can't discipline him. Professional help through your veterinarian, dog trainer and/or behaviorist can give you guidance.

Digging

Bored dogs release their frustrations through mischievous behavior such as digging. Dogs shouldn't be left unattended outside, even if they are in a fenced-in yard. Usually the dog is sent to "jail" (the backyard) because the owner can't tolerate him in the house. The culprit feels socially deprived and needs to be included in the owner's life. The owner has neglected the dog's training. The dog has not developed into the companion we desire. If you are one of these owners, then perhaps it is possible for you to change. Give him another chance. Some owners object to their dog's unkempt coat and doggy odor. See that he is groomed on a regular schedule and look into some training classes.

Submissive Urination

This is not a housebreaking problem. It can occur in all breeds and may be more

Bull Terriers possess innate curiosity and can "fall" into all sorts of predicaments. Be sure to supervise your dog at all times.

prevalent in some breeds. Usually it occurs in puppies but occasionally it occurs in older dogs and may be in response to physical praise. Try verbal praise or ignoring your dog until after he has had a chance to relieve himself. Scolding will only make the problem worse. Many dogs outgrow this problem.

Coprophagia

Also know as stool eating, sometimes occurs without a cause. It may begin with boredom and then becomes a habit that is hard to break. Your best remedy is to keep the puppy on a leash and keep the yard picked up. Then he won't have an opportunity to get in trouble. Your veterinarian can dispense a medication that is put on the dog's food that makes the stool taste bitter. Of course this will do little good if your dog cleans up after other dogs.

There are many predicaments your Bull Terrier puppy can get into the great outdoors. Always supervise him closely when outside.

The Runaway

There is little excuse for a dog to run away since dogs should never be off leash except when supervised in the fenced-in yard.

Many prospective owners that want to purchase a female since a male is inclined to roam. It is true that an intact male is inclined to roam, which is one of the reasons a male should be neutered. However, females will roam also, especially if they are in heat. Regardless, these dogs should never be given this opportunity. A few years ago one of our clients elected euthanasia for her elderly dog that radiographically appeared to have an intestinal blockage. The veterinarian suggested it might be a corncob. She assured him that was not possible since they hadn't had any. Apparently he roamed and raided the neighbor's garbage and you guessed it—he had a corncob blocking his intestines. Another dog raided the neighbor's garbage and died from toxins from the garbage.

To give the benefit of the doubt, perhaps your dog escapes or perhaps you are playing with your dog in the yard and he refuses to come when called. You now have a runaway. Help!

The first thing to remember is when you finally do catch your naughty dog, you must not discipline him. The reasoning behind this is that it is quite possible there could be a repeat performance, and it would be nice if the next time he would respond to your sweet command.

Always kneel down when trying to catch the runaway. Dogs are afraid of people standing over them. Also it would be helpful to have a treat or a favorite toy to help entice him to your side. After that initial runaway experience, start practicing the recall with your dog. You can let him drag a long line (clothesline) and randomly call him and then reel him in. Let him touch you first. Reaching for the dog can frighten him. Each time he comes you reward him with a treat and eventually he should get the idea that this is a nice experience. The long line prevents him from really getting out of hand. At least with the long line you can step on it and stop him.

Food Guarding

If you see signs of your puppy guarding his food, then you should take immediate steps to correct the problem. It is not fair to your puppy to feed him in a busy environment where children or other pets may interfere with his eating. This can be the cause of food guarding. Puppies should be fed in their crates where they do not feel threatened. Another advantage of this is that the puppy gets down to the business of eating and doesn't fool around. Perhaps you have seen possessiveness over the food bowl or his toys. Start by feeding him out of your hand and teach him that it is okay for you to remove his food

Food guarding can be a sign of dominant behavior in your dog. Discourage this by feeding him in an area where he will not be distracted from his meal.

bowl or toy and that you most assuredly will return it to him. If your dog is truly a bad actor and intimidates you, try keeping him on leash and perhaps sit next to him making happy talk. At feeding time make him work for his reward (his dinner) by doing some obedience command such as sit or down. Before your problem gets out of control you should get professional help. If he is out of control over toys, perhaps you should dispose of them or at least put them away when young children are around.

Your Bull Terrier is happiest when being loved and enjoyed. Although correction will sometimes be necessary, it will all prove worthwhile in the end.

Mischief and Misbehavior

All puppies and even some adult dogs will get into mischief at some time in their lives. You should start by "puppy proofing" your house. Even so it is impossible to have a sterile environment. For instance, if you would be down to four walls and a floor your dog could still chew a hole in the wall. What do you do? Remember puppies should never be left unsupervised so let us go on to the trusted adult dog that has misbehaved. His behavior may be an attention getter. Dogs, and even children, are known to do mischief even though they know they will be punished. Your puppy/dog will benefit from more attention and new direction. He may benefit from a training class or by reinforcing the obedience he has already learned. How about a daily walk? That could be a good outlet for your dog, time together and exercise for both of you.

Separation Anxiety

This occurs when dogs feel distress or apprehension when separated from their owners. One of the mistakes owners make is to set their dogs up for their departure. Some authorities recommend paying little attention to the pet for at least ten minutes before leaving and for the first ten minutes after you arrive home. The dog isn't cued to the fact you are leaving and if you keep it lowkey they learn to accept it as a normal everyday occurrence. Those dogs that are used to being crated usually accept your departure. Dogs that are anxious may have a serious problem and wreak havoc on the house within a few minutes after your departure. You can try to acclimate your dog to the separation by leaving for just a few minutes at a time, returning and rewarding him with a treat. Don't get too carried away. Plan on this process taking a long time. A behaviorist can set down a schedule for you. Those dogs that are insecure, such as ones obtained from a humane shelter or those that have changed homes, present more of a problem.

Punishment

A puppy should learn that correction is sometimes necessary and should not question your authority. An older dog that has never received correction may retaliate. In my opinion there will be a time for physical punishment but this does not mean hitting the dog. Do not use newspapers, fly swatters, etc. One type of correction, that is used by the mother dog when she corrects her puppies, is to take the puppy by the scruff and shake him *gently*. For the older, larger dog you can grab the scruff, one hand on each side of his neck, and lift his legs off the ground. This is effective since dogs feel intimidated when their feet are off the ground. Timing is of the utmost importance when punishment is necessary. Depending on the degree of fault, you might want to reinforce punishment by ignoring your dog for 15 to 20 minutes. Whatever you do, do not overdo corrections or they will lose value.

The most important advice to you is to be aware of your dog's actions. Even so, remember dogs are dogs and will behave as such even though we might like them to be perfect little people. You and your dog will become neurotic if you worry about every little indiscretion. When there is reason for concern—don't waste time. Seek guidance. Dogs are meant to be loved and enjoyed.

References:

Manual of Canine Behavior, Valerie O'Farrell, British Small Animal Veterinary Association.

Good Owners, Great Dogs, Brian Kilcommons, Warner Books.

SUGGESTED READING

TS-214
Skin & Coat Care For
Your Dog
432 pages, over 300
full-color photos

TS-249
Owner's Guide to Dog
Health
224 pages, over 190
full-color photos

TS-252
Dog Behavior and
Training
292 pages, over 200 full-
color photos

TS-257
Choosing A Dog For Life
384 pages, over 700 full-
color photos

INDEX